METHUEN'S OLD ENGLISH LIBRARY

General Editors

A. H. Smith
Quain Professor of English, University College, London

and

F. Norman
Professor of German, King's College, London

★

THE PARKER
CHRONICLE

THE PARKER
CHRONICLE
832-900

Edited by
A. H. SMITH, Ph.D.

NEW YORK
APPLETON-CENTURY-CROFTS
Division of Meredith Publishing Company

First published in the U.S.A. 1966

Printed in Great Britain

PREFACE

THE object of this edition is to present a reliable text of a section of the oldest manuscript of the Chronicle. A complete section such as this will give a much clearer picture of the structure of the Chronicle than isolated and disconnected selections. It is true that in this way some interesting passages (such as the Cynewulf-Cyneheard episode) are omitted, but the possibility of a reasonable estimate of the historical value of the Chronicle and the possibility of a fair appraisement of its literary qualities are important gains. The particular portion printed here covers the earliest Danish invasions and Ælfred's reign and is the work of several almost contemporary scribes. The scope of the edition is limited by the amount of original text, for many of the major problems involve a study of all manuscripts of the Chronicles. Some effort has been made, however, to indicate in the introduction and notes what these problems are. The constant reference to the works of Mawer, Beaven, Stenton and above all of Plummer will shew to what extent I, like all other students of the Chronicles, am indebted to these scholars. I am indebted to Sir Edwyn Hoskyns, Bt., Librarian of Corpus Christi College, Cambridge, for allowing me access to the manuscript, and my thanks are due to Professor Bruce Dickins for some valuable suggestions and for reading the proofs, as well as to Professor R. W. Chambers and Professor E. V. Gordon.

A. H. SMITH

UNIVERSITY COLLEGE, LONDON
January 1935

DANISH CAMPAIGNS 865-879

Movement of the army led by
Ragnar Lodbrok's sons
865-873 to Repton
Halfdene's campaign 873-875
Guthrum's campaign 873-876
Campaign 876-879
Centres and dates of
settlements
Danish winter quarters
Places on routes
of Danish armies
Southern limit of
Danelaw (885)
Modern County
boundaries

STRATHCLYDE

NORTHUMBRIA

Nb
874
Du
Cu
We
YN
York
875
866
868
YE
La
YW
Ch
Db
Torksey
872
L
MIDDLE
ANGLIA
Nt
876
Repton
873
Nottingham
867
Lei
R
EAST
ANGLIA
Sa
St
Nf
865
Wa
Nth
Hu
Thetford
C 869
Sf
879
Wo
Bd
Cambridge
874
He
Hrt
Gl
Cirencester
878
O
Bk
Ess
Chippenham
Ashdown
Mx
London
877
Brk
Reading
871
Edington
870
KENT
W
Basing
Wedmore
So
Sr
Aller
Iley
Wilton
Ha
X
Sx
D
Do
W
E
S
S
E
Exeter
876
Wareham
875
Co

Scale of Miles
0   20   40   60   80   100

CONTENTS

ABBREVIATIONS

Beaven	. .	M. L. R. Beaven, EHR xxxiii. 328–42 (1918)
BT	. .	J. Bosworth and T. N. Toller, *An Anglo-Saxon Dictionary*, 1882, 1921
EETS .	.	Early English Text Society (Original Series)
EHR .	.	English Historical Review
EPN .	.	English Place-Name Society publications
ESt	. .	Englische Studien
Hoffmann·Hirtz	.	M. Hoffmann-Hirtz, *Une Chronique Anglo-Saxonne*, 1933
Mawer .	.	A. Mawer, *Palaestra* cxlvii (1925)
ME	. .	Middle English
MLN .	.	Modern Language Notes
NED .	.	New English Dictionary
ODan .	.	Old Danish
OE	. .	Old English
OET .	.	H. Sweet, *Oldest English Texts*, 1885
OIcel .	.	Old Icelandic
ON	. .	Old Norse
Plummer	.	C. Plummer, *Two of the Saxon Chronicles Parallel*, 1892–9
Stevenson	.	W. H. Stevenson, *Asser's Life of Alfred*, 1904
Thorpe	.	B. Thorpe, *The Anglo-Saxon Chronicle*, 1861
WSax .	.	West Saxon

THE
PARKER CHRONICLE

INTRODUCTION

THE ultimate origin of the type of historical composition represented by the Old English Chronicles
is probably to be sought in the Easter Tables *
which were drawn up to assist the clergy to determine the
date of this great Christian festival in any year in an era.
The tables were generally arranged with the year of the
era and the figures for determining the date of Easter on
a single line, and with their ample margins they provided
a suitable framework into which short historical notices
could be fitted, not as the basis of a contemporary history, but to distinguish the years from one another as
they receded and grew confused in memory. Moreover,
the Easter Tables required and gave rise to an era or
system of reckoning by years which was also necessary before anything in the way of historical annals could be
attempted.†

The difference between the primitive type of annal,
which was nothing more than a short notice opposite the

---

* This problem is considered by R. L. Poole, *Chronicles and
Annals* (Oxford 1926). See also Plummer II. cxiv.

† On the general problem of the development of the Christian
era out of the cycle of years invented by Dionysus Exiguus in 525
as the basis of an Easter Table, see R. L. Poole, *Medieval Reckonings
of Time* (1921), 39 ff. Dionysus uses one of the dates computed
as the year of Christ's birth as a starting-point for a series of years
to accompany his Easter Table. This series of years was first
used as an era in England in the late seventh century and largely
through the popularity of Bede's work it became the recognized
system.

year-number in an Easter Table, and the Old English
Chronicles is largely one of intention. The Chronicles aim
at being repositories of facts grouped together in years.
They are long past the stage of the single-line entry, but
the first scribe of the Parker MS was still influenced by these
primitive annals when he wrote a series of year-numbers
on successive lines on the assumption that a single line
would suffice for each year—only to find that he needed
two or more. This explains why some of the annals are
opposite several year-numbers.*

In the Chronicle facts are related impersonally, except-
ing, perhaps, the outburst in 896, *Næfde se here, Ɉodes
ponces, Anɉelcyn ealles forspiðe ɉebrocod*. And similarly
apart from one or two references to preceding annals, as
for example the repeated allusions to the date the great
Danish army came into this country,† there is no attempt
to relate these facts to one another or to inquire into their
causes. The material is uneven, sometimes an important
fact is missing, and, as will be seen below (pp. 9 ff), the
chronology itself is occasionally uncertain. In spite of
these defects the Old English Chronicles remain the most
fruitful source for the history of England between Bede
and the Norman Conquest. Besides this, the fact that
they are vernacular compositions and, in the later years,
at all events, not based upon Latin writings, gives them
additional value, for in them we have the best examples
of early Old English prose. Occasionally the style is
clumsy and ambiguous (cf, for example, 837^5, 871^{25}, 871^{39},
893^8), but usually the meaning is clearly and definitely
expressed and there is some variety in the mode of expression (cf below, p. 14).

VERSIONS AND ORIGIN OF THE CHRONICLE

There are seven extant manuscripts of the Chronicles,
falling, as Plummer shews, into four distinct groups ‡ :

---

* Cf textual notes to 833, 840, 860, below.
† Cf 893^1, 893^{99}, 894^{16}, 895^1, 895^{22}, &c, also 892^1.
‡ Plummer II. xxiii ff.

I. MS A¹ (the Parker MS), formerly Archbishop Parker's, now Corpus Christi College, Cambridge, MS 173, folios 1–32, followed by the Acts of Lanfranc, the Laws of Ine and Ælfred, &c. The text of the present edition is derived from this MS. For the years covered by the present text the following hands may be noted. The first hand continues to the foot of fol. 16a (see notes p. 40) ; the second hand starts on fol. 16b and, according to Thorpe I. 162 and Plummer I. 85n, II. xxv, finishes at the bottom of this fol. 16b in the middle of a sentence which is carried on by the third hand on fol. 17a * ; the third hand finishes at the bottom of fol. 17b. The fourth hand starts on fol. 18a and this is the last hand until after 900. The first scribe may well have completed his section about the year 891, and there is nothing in the character of the remaining hands to shew that they do not belong approximately to the period covered by their particular entries, though on purely palaeographical grounds they might belong to any period in the tenth century. Besides the main hands, there are interpolations by later scribes, and where these can be definitely ascribed to later hands they are printed in italics in the present edition. Whatever the origin of the manuscript (see below, p. 8), it was

* It is not certain from the general character or details of penmanship that the ' second ' and ' third ' hands of Plummer's list (II. xxv), followed by M. R. James, *A Descriptive Catalogue of the MSS in Corpus Christi College, Cambridge*, 1912, I. 396, are to be considered different. The only difference is that the second scribe was cramming matter on fol. 16b ; fol. 16, it should be noted, is the last folio of the second gathering (cf Plummer II. xxiv, M. R. James, *op. cit.* I. 395). When the second scribe took up the MS he would have only one page to fill up at the end of the original MS ; he may, not unnaturally, have crammed matter on this page and he certainly followed the punctures made by the first scribe on fol. 16a as guide marks for the disposition of his lines, for the lines on fol. 16b coincide exactly with those on fol. 16a. But this scribe would have felt disposed to more spacious writing in his new gathering on fol. 17a, as his ascenders and descenders have more length than those of the original scribe of the Parker MS. It may be added that the MS is now so tightly bound and the head- and tail-bands fit so closely that it is not possible to check the collation.

certainly kept at Winchester in the tenth century, for entries with a particular Winchester interest are confined to the tenth century (see Plummer II. xcv). In the eleventh century this manuscript was transferred to Canterbury where many of the Kentish interpolations were made (as 870[6], 890[9]).

MS A[2], British Museum, Cotton MS Otho B XI, which was almost completely destroyed in the fire of 1731; Wheloc based his edition of the Chronicle on this manuscript, and the extant remains have been printed by K. Horst in ESt xxii. 447–450, xxv. 195. Recently a sixteenth-century transcript of the complete manuscript has come into the possession of the British Museum (Add. MS 43703), an account of which will appear in Dr. R. Flower's edition in this series of an hitherto unpublished Old English poem on Fasting. MS A[2] was a transcript of A[1] probably made at Winchester in the eleventh century, though M. Kupferschmidt on rather slender grounds attempts to make out a more elaborate relationship (ESt xiii. 165–187).

II. A lost chronicle similar to A[1], sent possibly to Abingdon, where some of the official continuations and a Mercian Register were incorporated:

MS B, British Museum, Cotton MS Tiberius A VI, is a copy of this chronicle made about 1000 and subsequently kept at Canterbury but without additions;

MS C, British Museum, Cotton MS Tiberius B I, is a mid-eleventh century copy of the lost Abingdon chronicle which had been kept up to date; MS C was itself kept up to 1066.

III. A copy of the original chronicle sent to the North was expanded by materials from Bede and other early northern sources, and it was kept up with additional northern material and the official continuations:

MS D, British Museum, Cotton MS Tiberius B IV, is a mid-eleventh century transcript of a copy of this northern chronicle which had been sent to the Worcester diocese; MS D was then continued to 1079.

IV. A chronicle which was akin to the northern ancestor of MS D but which did not incorporate all the West Saxon continuations was compiled and sent to Canterbury where it was kept till after the Conquest :

MS E (the ' Laud manuscript '), Bodleian MS, Laud 636, was a transcript of this Canterbury chronicle made at Peterborough about 1122 and there continued independently till 1154 ;

MS F, British Museum, Cotton MS Domitian A VIII, is a bilingual (English and Latin) epitome of this same Canterbury chronicle, made at Canterbury after the Conquest.*

The growth of these four groups of Chronicles may be shortly stated in this way : in the ninth century, a chronicle (not extant) was drawn up in Wessex from numerous sources, some of which have been identified † ; other sources are postulated to account for other material ; thus the comparative frequency of West Saxon entries down to 754 and a paucity of such entries for the period 755–823 suggests that the compiler had a set of West Saxon annals down to the year 754 ; the five West Saxon entries between 755 and 823 may in a few cases have been derived from oral, but in other cases written, tradition.‡ After 823, the English material is contemporary with the compilation

---

* With the exception of F all these versions have been printed at various times ; the most important editions are Thorpe's (which prints A¹, B, C, D, E, and parts of F, sometimes with silent alterations of the MSS), Plummer's (which prints MSS A¹ and E in full, with occasional extracts from the rest) and Classen and Harmer (MS D, very carefully reproduced) ; Plummer's is the standard text, but there are some errors of transcription, such as 836 *fultumode* (MS *fultomode*), 837¹ *aldorman* (MS *aldormon*), 840 *wælstowe* (MS *pelstope*), 887¹⁸ *drefde* (MS *dræfde*), 890 *butueoh* (MS *betueoh*), 894⁷ *sio* (MS *seo*), 894¹⁴, 895¹ *ylcan* (MS *ilcan*), 895⁶ *þare* (MS *þære*), 895⁹ *þe þære eǽ* (MS *þi þære éæ*), 895¹⁴ *scypu* (MS *scipu*), 896²⁵ *mycel* (MS *micel*), 896³⁹ *eodan* (MS *eodon*), 896⁵² *þam* (MS *þæm*), &c.

† Such as Bede's *Historia Ecclesiastica* and its chronological summary (Bk V, cap. xxiv), a continuation of this down to Ecgberht, genealogical lists of Northumbrian and Mercian kings, &c ; cf Plummer II. cix.

‡ Cf H. M. Chadwick, *Origin of the English Nation* (Cambridge 1924) 26, and F. P. Magoun, Anglia xlv. 24 ff.

of the original chronicle in the sense that it was incorporated within living memory of the events. The records of foreign events, especially for the years 880–c.890, may have been drawn from contemporary continental annals.

The date when this original chronicle was compiled is uncertain. The first hand of MS A[1] carries us down to the year 891 ; this scribe adds the year-number 892 but made no entry (see notes *infra*, p. 40) ; the annal 891 was completed later by the second scribe. This suggests that 891 was the date when the first part of the Parker MS was written and therefore the latest at which the original chronicle could have been compiled. Certainly up to this point all the extant versions have a common source. But there may have been still earlier recensions. There was possibly one which finished at 887, for Asser only uses a version of the Chronicle down to that year.[*] There was possibly an older version still, for the genealogy of Æþelwulf given immediately after the death of Æþelwulf in the annal 855 looks like the termination of such a recension,[†] which was brought up to date in Ælfred's reign and carried on at intervals to 891. It is almost impossible to reconstruct the character of the lost original, whatever its date, for not even the oldest of the extant versions, the Parker MS, gives by itself a clear picture of its prototype,[‡] whilst it seems likely that a version of the Chronicle

[*] Cf M. L. R. Beaven, EHR xxxiii. 331, n. 13. If this is true, then material must have been added to the annal 887, which in its extant form could not have been written before Spring 889 (cf notes to 887 *infra*, p. 38).

[†] Cf F. M. Stenton, *Essays presented to T. F. Tout* (Manchester 1925), 15, note 2. Professor Stenton says, on the other hand, that it is hard to believe that the ' hallowing ' of Ælfred as king (in 853) could have been recorded before Ælfred's accession in 871. But this is only a difficulty if we accept the chronicler's statement at its face value ; see, however, 853[8] (note).

[‡] The Parker MS has several errors, such as *Cariei* for *Caziei* (887) and some omissions (in 853, 874), and in 851 it arranges its material in a different order from the other MSS. That A[1] is a copy (to 891) is proved by the scribal error in 845 (see textual note to 845).

used by Ethelwerd contained more material than any of the extant manuscripts.*

The version of the Chronicle drawn up in Ælfred's reign has long been associated by scholars with Ælfred and Winchester. This version, as we have seen, belongs to 887, or at the latest to 891, and as Ælfred is known to have inspired literary activity about that time he may well have ordered an older recension of the chronicle to be brought up to date. But the only evidence we have is in the twelfth-century Gaimar's *L'Estorie des Engles* (ed. T. D. Hardy, Rolls Series, I., ll. 3451-2), *Il fist escrivere un livre Engleis Des aventures e des leis.* From the association of the annals with the laws, Plummer (II. cv, note) rightly concluded that Gaimar knew a manuscript of the Chronicle like A[1] where the Chronicle and the Laws are found together. That the attribution to Ælfred should be found only in the version of the Chronicle to which Gaimar had access is unlikely and it is probably no more than a guess by Gaimar based upon his knowledge that the Laws were called the Laws of Ælfred. A further connexion with Ælfred has also been suggested on the grounds of close verbal parallels between the Chronicle and the Old English Orosius,† but these parallels are such as would be expected in works with similar themes, and in any case many of them are found in the post-Ælfredian section. At the most these similarities of expression could only prove that the Chronicler and the translator of the Orosius were familiar with each other's work. Furthermore, Ælfred may not have stood alone in his patronage of learning and literature ; ' personal reasons, not now to be discovered, may have led some particular noble of the ninth century to wish for a vernacular rendering of earlier English history '.‡ The objections raised are against the type of evidence used to prove that Ælfred

---

* Cf F. M. Stenton, *op. cit.* 20-1.

† Plummer II. cvi-cvii. Those in the annals 832-900 are cited in the notes to 865, 867, 871, 879, 891, 893.

‡ F. M. Stenton, *op. cit.* 23.

himself wrote the Chronicle ; such objections, however, cannot prove and, indeed, are not intended to prove that Ælfred could not have been the compiler. He may have participated in the compilation of the Chronicle, but we cannot prove it. At the same time, it seems likely that he should have sponsored it in some way or other. The textual history of the different versions suggests that the ' Ælfredian ' Chronicle was circulated throughout the kingdom, and on the analogy of the *Cura Pastoralis* (cf below, p. 9 note) it is likely, as an ' official ' document, to have had the king's sanction.

The association of the original chronicle with Winchester is equally uncertain. The chief evidence is again provided by Gaimar,* whose statement was without doubt based upon the view (also held by some modern writers) that Winchester was Ælfred's capital. It is commonly held † that Winchester was the ' national ' capital as well as the ecclesiastical centre of Wessex and therefore the likely home of a ' national ' chronicle. But in a very lucid discussion of this problem Professor Stenton (*op. cit.* 15 ff) has shewn that the importance of Winchester belongs to the tenth and eleventh centuries, not the ninth, and that in the ninth century it is improbable that Wessex had any definite capital. Moreover, the chronicle as we know it is far from being a ' national ' chronicle—a character ascribed to it, perhaps, to explain the infrequency of Winchester entries (855 and 860 are amongst the few). On the contrary, the local interest is at times strongly developed, but then it is always centred on Dorset and

---

* *Croniz ad nun, un livere grant : Engleis l'alerent asemblant. Ore est issi auctorizez, Ka Wincestre, en l'eveskez, La est des reis la dreite estorie E les vies e la memorie* (Gaimar, *ed. cit.* ll. 2331–6). Cf also Plummer II. cxii. Earle (in his edition of the Chronicle, p. xi) supposed that the association with Winchester is strengthened by the regular record of the Bishops of Winchester 634–754. This, however, is probably derived from an independent series of West Saxon annals (cf above, p. 5, and H. M. Chadwick, *op. cit.* 26). It is significant that the series is broken at 754.

† Plummer II. cxii; A. Brandl, *Pauls Grundriss* III. 1057, 1071.

Somerset; it is observed mainly in the preservation of names of obscure places and persons from this south-western region (cf 845, 851, and especially 878), but perhaps more significant is the annal 867 recording the death of Ealhstan, bishop of Sherborne; the annal adds that ' his body lies there *on tune* ', a detail which only an annalist knowing Sherborne well would find of enough interest to insert in his chronicle.* On such grounds it is not unreasonable to suppose that the Ælfredian recension of the Chronicle was made in the south-west and that copies were circulated from there to different parts of the country † ; that is why there is so much resemblance between some of the extant versions down to about 891. Sometimes, these copies were revised with the incorporation of local material. From time to time new contemporary matter was officially circulated, occasionally supplemented by local information. Fresh copies were made and sent to other places where new local material was added, and no doubt these localized versions were used to bring up to date copies in other places. The manuscripts that have survived are for the most part transcripts of such copies and from these circumstances their textual relationship is complex. There is, however, contemporary or nearly contemporary material of the ninth and tenth centuries in MS A[1], and of the eleventh and twelfth centuries in MS E.

CHRONOLOGY

It might be expected that a chronicle which takes an order of years for its framework would be accurate in its chronological information, but such is not the case with the

* Cf also 878[17] note.

† The circulation of manuscripts of the Chronicle would be analogous to the distribution of copies of the *Cura Pastoralis* intended by Ælfred : *to ælcum biscepstole on minum rice wille* [ic] *ane onsendan* (ed. H. Sweet, EETS xlv, 6). It is quite possible that the Parker MS itself down to 891 was such a copy made in the south-west ; it becomes a chronicle with a Winchester interest only after 891 (see above, p. 3).

Old English Chronicle. In the series of annals 754–845 the events are recorded two years and in some annals (829–39, possibly to 845) three years too early. This error was not in the original version, for an archaic manuscript of the chronicle used in the Annals of St Neots was apparently free from it * ; but since it appears in all extant manuscripts of the chronicle it was no doubt made in an early recension, where the scribe wrongly omitted to pass over two annals 754 and 756 for which there should have been no entries. The error is corrected at 851, as a series of blank annals 846–50 made a return to the true chronology possible.

A second error whereby events are recorded one year too late occurs in the annals 892–928 in MS A[1] only. The original scribes copied the annals under the proper years, but in the tenth century mistaken ' corrections ' were made by scribes who added 1 to each of the dominical years in this series.†

A third set of inconsistencies in dating events is more complex, but an explanation has been put forward in a very scholarly fashion by the late M. L. R. Beaven,‡ to shew why only certain events in an annal appear to be recorded a year too late. Actually the annalistic year under which an event was recorded depended upon the date at which the annalist's year began. In mediaeval times the year could begin (in relation to our present practice of starting it on 1 January) on (1) the Annunciation (25 March) preceding 1 January (the so-called *Stylus Pisanus*), (2) 1 September preceding 1 January (the Constantinople Indiction), (3) 24 September preceding

* Cf L. Theopold, *Kritische Untersuchungen* (1872), 53, 85, Plummer II. cii, ciii, and Stevenson 105–6.

† See notes to 891 [14], 892, below. In this edition the dates given by the original scribes have been restored, 892 being treated as part of the annal 891, 893 as 892, and so on. Similarly all references are to these restored dates. This has so far been done by only one scholar, Professor R. W. Chambers, in his *England before the Norman Conquest* (1926).

‡ EHR xxxiii. 328–42.

1 January (the Caesarean Indiction), (4) 25 December (Christmas Day, Mid-Winter's Day) before 1 January, (5) 1 January, and (6) the Annunciation after 1 January (the *Stylus Florentinus*).* Of these possible beginnings Bede and the older parts of the Chronicle use the Caesarean Indiction of 24 September, and from about 890 the Chronicle also uses the Christmas beginning (see notes *ad loc.*), but not exclusively (cf 900 note). These facts are not self-evident, for only by correlation with data from other sources can the obscure chronology of the Chronicle be explained. The relevant difficulties are these: from 878 foreign events are often recorded one year too late; thus the autumnal movement of the Danes to Ghent recorded under 880 belongs to November 879, the movement to the Meuse recorded in 882 to November 881, and so on (see notes to 880, 881, 882, 883, 884, 885 and 885[15], 886[2], 887, 890[6]). Earle and Plummer, who assumed a Christmas beginning for most parts of the Chronicle, suggested that this series of annals 879–87 (see 879 n) was one year out, but this took no account of foreign events which are correctly dated in those annals, as, for example, the Battle with the Franks of August 881, correctly recorded under 881. If, however, the year began at the September Indiction events which took place between 24 September and 31 December would naturally be entered under what is to us the following year. The evidence for such a beginning is clear. In many of the annals the first recorded event is the autumnal movement of the Danes into winter-quarters. Again, in the annal 885 the death of Louis is said to have occurred in the year of the sun's eclipse, the eclipse being already recorded under 879. This eclipse was on 29 October, 878, and Louis' death on 10 April,

* See further R. L. Poole, *The Beginning of the Year in Mediæval Times* (Proceedings of the British Academy, X (1921), (reprinted in R. L. Poole, *Studies in Chronology and History*, (Oxford) 1934); R. L. Poole, *Medieval Reckonings of Time*, 1918. Plummer also assumes an Easter beginning, but the instances given by him are merely examples of the Stylus Florentinus (cf Beaven 329).

879 (see notes to 879, 885[15]) ; these two dates were clearly within one annalistic year, which must therefore have commenced between 11 April and 28 October. Similarly the chronological details in the annal 871 shew that the year began between the end of May and 28 December and those in 878 that it began between 6 July and 7 January (see notes to 878[1], 878[10]) ; the final events in the annal 877 carry the earlier limiting date to 7 August (see note to 877[10]). Putting this evidence together, we can determine that the year began somewhere between 7 August and 28 October; we may guess that the year actually began at the Caesarean Indiction of 24 September, for there is no evidence that the Constantinople Indiction of 1 September was ever used in England.

This establishment of the beginning of the annalist's year does not materially alter the chronological development of Ælfred's campaigns, but it does explain inconsistencies in the recording of foreign events and some obscurities in the movements of the Danes. It enables us, for example, to put the first wintering of the Danes in Thanet recorded in 851 in the late autumn of 850 and therefore before their defeat at *Aclea* in 851 ; this defeat was so overwhelming that nothing more is heard of the Danes until 853, and meanwhile Burȝred of Mercia and king Æþelwulf subdued the Welsh. It is unlikely that this Welsh campaign would have been attempted had the defeated Danes gone into winter-quarters in the autumn of 851. Other annals which also become clearer in the light of an annalistic year beginning on 24 September are 868, 870, 872, 874, 878, 879, 900.

LANGUAGE OF THE PARKER MS

The orthography and phonology of the Parker MS throws little light on its place of origin, but judging by the preservation of occasional archaisms in proper names drawn from versions of the Chronicle used by Asser and in the Annals of St Neots,* the Parker MS down to 891 was a somewhat modernized version ; it is thus one of the principal sources for the study of West Saxon of the second half of the ninth century.

The most significant feature is the change of orthography that accompanied a change in handwriting. In the first hand down to 891, ð is almost unknown (broður 871, ðeron 882, ðæm 891), þ being the usual symbol ; ð is found more frequently after 891 and becomes common in 894. The letter ę is usual down to 891, though æ is found occasionally and Ae once (Aelfred 885) ; æ only is used after 891. Other archaic spellings in the first hand include an occasional u, uu for p (cuom, tueʒen, uuoldon 878), and the frequent use of u for later o in unstressed syllables (ʒefenʒun 851, broþur 860, ʒebocude 855). Older phonological forms in the first hand include the retention of u in cuom (com in later hands, as 893), final ʒ remaining voiced in ofsloʒ 885 (later ofsloh), and the retention of the diphthong io (later eo), as in elþiodiʒnesse 891, sio 885 ; the second hand, it may be noted, has one or two io forms, as sio besides seo in 893. The characteristic West Saxon diphthong ie is found almost invariably down to 891, as unieþelice 878, aþiestrode 879, fierd, but after 891 later WSax or non-WSax variants are found, as uneðelice 896, fird 895. Before 891 a before l + consonant generally remains unbroken, as ʒepald 833, salde 836, aldormon 837, alle 853, haldanne 874, apart from a rare broken form like healdan 887, but after 891 broken forms are regular, as ealle 892, sealde 893, ealdormon 893, &c. The unbroken forms of the first hand may be Anglian in origin, due possibly to some Anglian scholar, who like Pleʒemund (see note to 890[9]) had sought patronage in Wessex, or they may be a relic of a more archaic WSax spelling tradition ;

* Cf Coenred (oe from i-mutation of ō, later ē) ; Guuihtgara-burhg (containing the old gen.sg. -gāra from -gār, an old u-stem, later -gares ; cf Parker MS þihtʒarasburʒ) ; Koenuualh (later Cēn-), Oisc (later replaced by Æsc). See Stevenson lxxxv, 105, 173.

but non-WSax forms are otherwise very rare * before
891 ; on the other hand, archaic spellings already noted,
as well as *efor* 885 (which would be archaic in any dialect),
support the second alternative.†

With the later hands the orthography is more varied
and though in the second hand there are a few stray
archaisms like *porhtun* (later *-on*), *ʒepaldenum* (later *-ea-*),
ʒeporct ‡ (later *-ht*) 893, there are many spellings usually
associated with WSax of the tenth century, as *sæde* (for
sæʒde) 893, *þena* (for *þeʒna* 896), *betpuh* 893 (cf *betueoh*
889), *pucena* 893 (cf older *piecan* 878), *cinʒes* 893 (older
cyninʒes), and occasional forms (besides those in *ie* already
mentioned) with diphthongs simplified (perhaps on Anglian
models), as *ʒeperc* 895, *þeh* (*conj.*) 893, 896, *mehte* 893, &c,
mehton 893, &c, *ʒere* 894, &c (cf *ʒepeorc* 868, *þeah* (*adv.*)
867, *meahte* 877, *ʒeare*).

In its style the Chronicle is generally clear and simple.
Through the recurrence of events of a similar kind there is
a tendency towards the constant use of stereotyped phrases
such as *ahton pælstope ʒepald*, *siʒe namon*, &c, but in spite
of this the diction is varied. Further, the traditional
notion of a chronicle would offer little scope for the skilful
and artistic unfolding of a story, but the exposition is not
monotonous, and for one of the earliest specimens of free

* The only noteworthy one is *piotan* 853, 868 (with Kentish or
Anglian back-mutation, WSax *pitan*)

† Unfortunately the evidence for very early WSax is scanty,
but, in the few charters, we have broken and unbroken forms in
proper names, as OET 427 no. 2 (693–731) *ualdharius* ; 427 no. 3
(778) *-healh*, *egcbaldus* ; 434 no. 20 (847) *denewaldes stan*, *fordealf*,
healdanweg, *wealdenesford*, *se alda suinhaga*, *alhstan*. The earliest
West Saxon orthography may have been modelled to a considerable
extent on Anglian. There is in later times no evidence to support
Luick's conjecture (*Historische Grammatik*, § 146 n. 2) that in
some WSax dialects there was sound-development similar to that
in Anglian.

‡ It is doubtful whether this is really archaic ; a simple spelling
mistake is more likely, for the scribe wrote *ʒepeorc* at the end of
fol. 17a and then wrote *ʒeporc* (for *ʒeporht*) at the beginning of
fol. 17b ; it was corrected by adding *t*. See textual note 893[59].

prose composition in the language and one largely independent of Latin influence the variety of expression and
the restraint shewn by the chronicler are remarkable.

The sentences, especially the compound sentences, are of a
primitive type ; parataxis is the rule and hypotaxis the exception.*
But although the style is simple and occasionally ambiguous, there
is a fair range in sentence-structures. The most characteristic
types include : (1) The simple sentence often introduced by an
adverb or adverbial expression with the finite verb before the
subject, as *Her for se here up on Sunnan* 884 or *þy ilcan ȝeare æt
middum pintra forþferde Carl Francna cyninȝ* 885, though where
the subject is plural the normal order of subject and predicate is
often kept, as *On þa ea hi tuȝon up hiora scipu* 892. (2) A succession
of such sentences joined by *ond*, as *7 þy ilcan ȝeare ȝebocude Æþelpulf cyninȝ teoþan dęl his londes... 7 þy ilcan ȝeare ferde to Rome....
7 þær pas xii monaþ puniende...* 855. (3) A rarer type of simple
sentence introduced by subject and predicate, as *Seo ea... lið ut
of þæm pealda* 892. (4) A simple sentence with the order of subject and finite verb reversed (rare), as *Næfde se here, ȝodes þonces,
Angelcyn ealles forspiþe ȝebrocod* 896, *Þæs Hæsten þa þær cumen.
Hæfde Hæsten ær ȝeporht þæt ȝepeorc* 893. (5) The common
type of compound or correlative sentence where the subordinate
clause is introduced by a conjunction with the subject and verb
in the order subject + verb and the principal sentence with or
without correlative adverb and subject and verb in reversed
order (as *Þa hie þa hampeard pendon, þa metton hie micelne
sciphere* 855. *Þa he þa pæs hiderpeardes 7 sio operu fierd hampeardes..., þa ȝeȝaderedon þa þe in Norþymbrum buȝeað....
sum hund scipa* 893).

---

* See G. Rübens, *Parataxe und Hypotaxe* (1915) ; the best study
of the style of the Chronicle is G. C. Donald, *Zur Entwicklung des
Prosastils in der Sachsenchronik* (1914).

A NOTE ON THE TEXT

The punctuation is modern. The use of capitals is modern (with a few exceptions capitals in the MS are confined to the first word of an annal) ; in proper names the MS normally uses small initials ; in this text Æ (initially in proper names) represents MS ę down to 891 (fol. 16a), thereafter æ. Abbreviations are expanded : ∼ as *m* (*nam*, MS *nā* 853[8] ; *hampeard*, MS *hāpeard* 855[6] ; &c) and as *n* rarely (*porhtun*, MS *porhtū* 893[68]) ; ' as *e* (ʒ' = ʒe, tpeʒ'n = tpeʒen ; moniʒ' = moniʒe 838[4] ; *fierd'* = *fierde* 851[10] ; *hæfd'* = *hæfde* 885[28] ; *h'* = *he* 878[29]) ; ' as *ep* (*bisc'(rice)* = *biscep(rice)* 845[2], 867[13] &c) ; ' as *er* (*pint'* = *pinter* 855[2] ; *æft'* = *æfter* 878[21] ; &c) and as *re* (*pint'* = *pintre* 870[2]) ; Latin words when abbreviated are expanded as in C. Trice Martin, *Record Interpreter* (London 1910). Additions above or below the line (as *ʒefeaht, t* above, 845 ; *fenʒon, on* above, 855[30] ; *adrencton, n* above *ct*, 890[9] ; *miercna, a* below, 851[9] ; *his, i* below, 851[10] ; &c) made by the original scribe of the particular annal are not noted except where the correction has interest. The year numbers (always Roman numerals) are usually in the left-hand margin as disposed in the printed text. In the text of the MS there is down to 891 no indentation by the year numbers ; as far as is consistent with economy of space, variations in the size of margin are indicated by spaces at the beginnings of the lines in this text. Some tribal names (*Sup-Seaxe, Norp-Ꝺalas*, &c) are hyphenated in this text ; the two elements are generally separate words in the MS.

THE PARKER CHRONICLE

(*Corpus Christi College, Cambridge, MS* 173, *fol.* 12a–20a)

Anno dcccxxxii. Her heþne men oferherʒeadon Sceapiʒe.
Anno dcccxxxiii. Her ʒefeaht Ecʒbryht cyninʒ þiþ xxxu
    sciphlæsta æt Carrum 7 þær pearþ micel þel ʒeslæʒen,
    7 þa Denescan ahton þelstope ʒepald ; 7 Hereferþ
    7 Þiʒþen tueʒen biscepas forþferdon, 7 Dudda 7
    Osmod tueʒen aldormen forþferdon.   5
Anno dcccxxxu. Her cuom micel sciphere on Þest-Þalas
    7 hie to anum ʒecierdon, 7 þiþ Ecʒbryht Þest
    Seaxna cyninʒ pinnende pæron. Þa he þæt hierde
    7 mid fierde ferde 7 him þiþ feaht æt Henʒestdune
    7 þær ʒefliemde ʒe þa Þalas ʒe þa Deniscan.   5

TEXTUAL VARIANTS : 833. Below 833 in margin is *Añ dcccxxxiiii*

---

832. Actually 835 (cf Introd. p. 9). Apart from the isolated
reference in 787, this is the first mention of the Danes in this version of the Chronicle. In 834 the Danes had been harrying in the
Netherlands (cf *Annales Xantenses*, ed. B. de Simson, Hannover
1909, p. 9), and the raid on Sheppey may have been made by the
same fleet. There was in later years a close connexion between
the English and Continental operations of the Danes (cf, for instance,
880, 885, 892).

833. Actually 836. 35 ship-crews would be about 700 to 1000
men ; *æt Carrum* is Carhampton, Somerset (cf B. Dickins, *Times
Literary Suppl.* 22 Sept. 1922, Mawer 46).

835. Actually 838. [2] *hie to anum ʒecierdon : hie* = the Cornish
and the Danes. On this and other alliances of the Cornish men
and the Danes cf B. G. Charles, *Old Norse Relations with Wales*
(Cardiff 1934), 2, and A. F. Major, *Early Wars of Wessex* (Cambridge 1913), 83. Cornwall hoped to throw off the Saxon domination, whilst it was not itself an attractive objective to the Danes
except for the men the latter could obtain for their raids on Wessex.

[3] *pinnende pæron :* note the progressive form ' continued fighting ' ; it is not frequent in OE ; cf also 867[7], 876.

17

Anno dcccxxxui. Her Ecȝbryht cyninȝ forþferde, 7 hine
    hæfde ær Offa Miercna cyninȝ 7 Beorhtric Þesseaxna
    cyninȝ afliemed xiii ȝear of Anȝelcynnes lande on
    Fronclond, ær he cyninȝ þære, 7 þy fultomode
    Beorhtric Offan þy he hæfde his dohtor him to   5
    cuene ; 7 se Ecȝbryht ricsode xxxuii þintra, uii
    monaþ, 7 fenȝ Æþelþulf Ecȝbrehtinȝ to Þesseaxna
    rice, 7 he salde his suna Æþelstane Cantþara rice
    7 East-Seaxna 7 Suþriȝea 7 Suþ-Seaxna.
Anno dcccxxxuii. Her Þulfheard aldormon ȝefeaht æt
    Hamtune þiþ xxxiii sciphlæsta 7 þær micel þæl
    ȝesloȝ 7 siȝe nom. 7 þy ȝeare forþferde Þulfheard.
    7 þy ilcan ȝeare ȝefeaht Æþelhelm dux þiþ Deniscne
    here on Port mid Dornsætum 7 ȝode hþile þone   5
    here ȝefliemde, 7 þa Deniscan ahton þælstope
    ȝeþald 7 þone aldormon ofsloȝon.

836³. *xiii*, MS *iii*. 836⁴. *þære* begins fol. 12b.

---

836. Actually 839. ² *hæfde :* note the singular form followed by
double subject, as in 875⁵. ² *ær....ær he cyninȝ þære,* ' on a pre-
vious occasion thirteen years before he was to be king '. On the
correction of MS *iii* to *xiii* cf Plummer II. 75.

⁸ *his suna Æþelstane,* Ecȝbryht's son Æþelstan.

837. Probably 840. ¹ *aldormon ;* the function of this high official
was to act as the king's principal deputy in a large district (cf H. M.
Chadwick, *Studies on Anglo-Saxon Institutions* (1905), 163, 282, 289).

⁵ *here,* hereafter the usual name for the Danish army ; in the
Laws of Ine a band of robbers numbering 7 to 35 was called a *hloþ*
(cf 893¹¹), and a band numbering 35 or more was called a *here*
(F. L. Attenborough, *Laws of the Earliest English Kings,* Cambridge
1922, p. 40).

⁵ 7 *ȝode hþile þone here ȝefliemde :* there is an apparent contra-
diction in the Danes being put to flight and yet gaining possession
of the battlefield ; so also in 871²⁵ ; cf Hoffmann-Hirtz 66n, G.
Rübens, *Parataxe und Hypotaxe* (1915), 20. MSS D and E substi-
tute for this another phrase (7 *se ealdorman þærð ofslæȝen*), which
makes the Danish victory clearer. In this version, however, the
passage probably means that ' for a long time they drove back
the Danes, but ultimately the Danes won the battle '. In the 871
example the same explanation may hold, but in anv case the language is there ambiguous.

Anno dcccxxxuiii.   Her Herebryht aldormon pæs ofslæȝen
    from heþnum monnum 7 moniȝe mid him on
    Merscparum, 7 þy ilcan ȝeare eft on Lindesse 7 on
    East-Enȝlum 7 on Cantparum purdon moniȝe men
    ofslæȝene from þam heriȝe.   5

Anno dcccxxxuiiii.   Her pæs micel pelsliht on Lundenne 7
    on Cpantapic 7 on Hrofesceastre.

Anno dcccxl.   Her Æþelpulf cyninȝ ȝefeaht æt Carrum piþ
    xxxu sciphlæsta,7 þa Deniscan a hton pelstope ȝepald.

Anno dcccxlu.   Her Eanulf aldorman ȝefeaht mid Sumur-
    sætum 7 Ealchstan biscep 7 Osric aldorman mid
    Dornsætum ȝefuhton æt Pedridan muþan piþ Den-
    iscne here 7 þær micel pel ȝesloȝon 7 siȝe namon.

840. The annal years in the margin are in an unbroken series to
852 ; the annal 840 takes 2 lines and is therefore opposite 840 and
841 ; 842, 843, 844 are blank ; the annal 845 in 3 lines is opposite
the year numbers 845, 846, 847 ; 848, 849, 850 are blank ; the first
two lines of the annal 851 are opposite the year numbers 851, 852.

845. A sentence has been erased at the end of this annal, but
enough remains to shew that the scribe has wrongly added here
the second sentence of 851, where it follows a sentence similar to
that in 845 ; the words now visible are | 7 þy ilcanȝ......þelstan......
ealchere dux......ofsloȝon | æt Sondpic on kent 7 uiiii scipu ȝefenȝun
7 þa oþre ȝefliemdon |.

---

838. Actually 841. Herebryht was an aldorman of Mercia and
Merscparum may refer to the ' people of the marshlands ' of Lincoln-
shire, rather than to Romney Marsh (Kent), suggested by Plummer
II. 412 ; eft in l. 3 may have the force of ' again in Lindsey '. But
Mersc (MS A), Merscpare (MS E &c) certainly refer to Romney
Marsh in 796.

839. Actually 842. Cpantapic, probably Quentowic, a lost place
near Étaples, destroyed by the Danes in 842 (Hoffmann-Hirtz
67n, Plummer II. 76).

840. Probably 843, or possibly 844 (according to L. Theopold,
Kritische Untersuchungen (1872), 61). From 843 to 848 the Danes
were engaged in raids on the Continent ; this probably explains
the absence of entries in the Chronicle between 840 and 845.
There is a great similarity between this annal and 833, but since
it is found in this form in all Chronicles there is no reason to doubt
its authenticity (cf Plummer II. 76).

845. Probably 848. æt Pedridan muþan, mouth of the R. Parrett, Somerset.

Anno dcccli. Her Ceorl aldormon ȝefeaht ƿiþ hæþene men mid Defenascire æt Ƿicȝanbeorȝe, 7 þær micel ƿæl ȝesloȝon 7 siȝe namon. 7 þy ilcan ȝeare Æþel- stan cyninȝ 7 Ealchere dux micelne here ofsloȝon æt Sondƿic on Cent 7 ix scipu ȝefenȝun 7 þa oþre ⁵ ȝefliemdon. 7 hæþne men ærest ofer ƿinter sæton. 7 þy ilcan ȝeare cuom feorðe healf hund scipa on Temese muþan 7 brecon Contparaburȝ 7 Lunden- burȝ, 7 ȝefliemdon Beorhtƿulf Miercna cyninȝ mid his fierde, 7 foron þa suþ ofer Temese on Suþriȝe ¹⁰ 7 him ȝefeaht ƿiþ Æþelƿulf cyninȝ 7 Æþelbald his sunu æt Aclea mid Ƿest-Seaxna fierde, 7 þær þæt mæste ƿæl ȝesloȝon on hæþnum heriȝe þe ƿe secȝan hierdon oþ þisne ondƿeardan dæȝ, 7 þær siȝe namon.

851⁷. *feorðe:* rðe added above the line by another hand; *eo* also appears to be a correction.   851¹⁴. MS 7 *ƿeardan.*

851. The true chronology is restored (see Introd. p. 10). The raid on Devonshire may have been a move to distract the West Saxons from the great invasion on the east (l. 6). But the fights at *Ƿicȝanbeorȝe* and Sandwich probably took place in the autumn of 850. The Danes then went into winter-quarters and in the spring of 851 the great invasion took place. The Danes were then defeated at *Aclea* and probably left the country (cf Introd. p. 12).

² *æt Ƿicȝanbeorȝe;* the identity is uncertain; Weekaborough (Devon) and Wigborough (Somerset) have been proposed and there is nothing in the early spellings of these names to rule out either (cf Stevenson 176, *Place-Names of Devon* (EPN IX), 506), though those of Wigborough agree more closely with *Ƿicȝanbeorȝe.* Wigborough is not in Devonshire, but it is only 5 miles outside and Stevenson (l.c.) notes that ' the *fyrd* is occasionally found fighting outside its county '.

⁸ *Lundenburȝ :* London was still under Mercian rule; it was recaptured by Ælfred in 886.

¹¹ *him ȝefeaht ƿiþ Æþelƿulf . . . :* as usual when the verb pre- cedes a multiple subject it takes the number of the first part of the subject ; cf 853¹ (see textual note to 853²), where a later scribe has added *bædon* as an alternative to the original singular form *bed.*

¹² *Aclea :* Ockley (Surrey) has been suggested by Plummer II. 78, but the early spellings of this name do not accord with *Aclea* (*Place-Names of Surrey* (EPN X), 208, 276). The name is common in OE and as the Chronicle gives no other clue the choice of the right Oakley must remain uncertain (Mawer 44).

Anno dcccliii. Her będ Burȝred Miercna cyninȝ 7 his
  piotan Æþelpulf cyninȝ þæt he him ȝefultumade
  þæt him Norþ-Palas ȝehiersumade. He þa spa
  dyde, 7 mid fierde fór ofer Mierce on Norþ-Palas,
  7 hie him alle ȝehiersume dydon. 7 þy ilcan ȝeare   5
  sende Æþelpulf cyninȝ Ælfred his sunu to Rome.
  Þa pas domine Leo papa on Rome, 7 he hine to
  cyninȝe ȝehalȝode 7 hiene him to biscepsuna nam.
  Þa þy ilcan ȝeare Ealhere mid Cantparum 7 Huda
  mid Suþriȝium ȝefuhton on Tenet piþ hęþnum   10
  heriȝe 7 ærest siȝe namon, 7 þær pearþ moniȝ
  mon ofslæȝen 7 adruncen on ȝehpęþere hond.
  Ond þæs ofer Eastron ȝeaf Æþelpulf cyninȝ his
  dohtor Burȝrede cyninȝe of Pesseaxum on Merce.
Anno dccclu. Her hęþne men ærest on Sceapiȝe ofer
  pinter sætun. 7 þy ilcan ȝeare ȝebocude Æþelpulf
  cyninȝ teoþan dęl his londes ofer al his rice Ȝode

853². ęþelpulf begins fol. 13a. In the margin is the date añ
dcccliiii; a later hand has added bædon above ęþelpulf; he, MS
he he. 853⁶. A cross in margin opposite Ælfred's name. 853⁷.
domine, papa, MS dõne, pãp. 853⁹. Huda mid, MS hudamid, with
a stroke below a to separate the words. 853¹⁴. Ond, MS O'.

855. On this and the next four lines of the margin of this annal
are the year numbers 855 to 859. 855³. Ȝode, MS ȝo.

853³. him may be singular ' him ' (i.e. Burȝred) or plural ' them '
(i.e. Burȝred and Æþelpulf in alliance).

⁸ to cyninȝe ȝehalȝode : Ælfred would now be 5 years old, for the
preface to the Chronicle says that he was 23 years old when he
became king in 871. The actual ceremony was apparently the
investing of Ælfred by Pope Leo IV with the robes and belt of consul
(see Leo's letter, cited by Plummer II. 79) and confirmation in the
faith. Perhaps the assertion that he was ' hallowed as king ' was
a misinformed rumour current in England, and possibly some such
report may have led to Æþelbald's revolt against his father Æþelwulf in 855 (Asser), about which the Chronicle is curiously silent.
Such a misunderstanding explains why Æþelbald could be granted
the rule of the western part of his father's kingdom after his revolt.

¹¹ ærest siȝe namon : it is not clear which side won.

¹⁴ of Pesseaxum . . . , ' as from Wessex to Mercia '.

855³. teoþan dęl his londes, ' a tenth part of his private lands ';
on this difficult problem cf Stevenson 186 ff. This annal summarizes
the rest of Æþelwulf's reign : his journey to Rome where he

21

to lofe 7 him selfum to ecere hęlo, 7 þy ilcan ʒeare
ferde to Rome mid micelre peorþnesse 7 þær pas ⁵
xii monaþ puniende 7 þa him hampeard fór, 7 him
þa Carl Francna cyninʒ his dohtor ʒeaf him to
cuene, 7 æfter þam to his leodum cuom 7 hie þæs
ʒefæʒene pærun. 7 ymb ii ʒear þæs ðe he of Francum com he ʒefór, 7 his lic liþ æt Þintanceastre, ¹⁰
7 he ricsode niʒonteoþe healf ʒear. Ond se Æþelpulf pæs Ecʒbrehtinʒ, Ecʒbryht Ealhmundinʒ,
Ealhmund Eafinʒ, Eafa Eoppinʒ, Eoppa Inʒildinʒ ;
Inʒild pæs Ines broþur Þest-Seaxna cyninʒes,
þæs þe eft ferde to Sancte Petre 7 þær eft his feorh ¹⁵
ʒesealde ; 7 hie pæron Cenredes suna, Cenred pæs
Ceolpaldinʒ, Ceolpald Cuþainʒ, Cuþa Cuþþininʒ,
Cuþþine Ceaulininʒ, Ceaplin Cynricinʒ, Cynric
Cerdicinʒ, Cerdic Elesinʒ, Elesa Eslinʒ, Esla Jipisinʒ,
Jipis Þiʒinʒ, Þiʒ Freapininʒ, Freapine Friþoʒarinʒ, ²⁰
Friþoʒar Brondinʒ, Brond Bęldæʒinʒ, Bęldæʒ
Þodeninʒ, Þoden Friþopaldinʒ, Friþupald Frea-
pininʒ, Frealaf Friþupulfinʒ, Friþupulf Finninʒ, Fin
Jodpulfinʒ, Jodpulf Jeatinʒ, Jeat Tętpainʒ, Tętpa
Beapinʒ, Beap Sceldpainʒ, Sceldpea Heremodinʒ, ²⁵
Heremod Itermoninʒ, Itermon Hraþrainʒ, se pæs
ʒeboren in þære earce : Noe, Lamach, Matusalem,

855⁹. of, MS on.   855¹¹. Ond, MS O'.
855¹⁸. Cuþþine, originally cuþa, a being underdotted and then
erased and þine added above the line.

---

remained till 856, his return through France where he contracted
a nominal political marriage with Judith, the twelve-year-old daughter of Carloman, his welcome home (in spite of Æþelbald's revolt),
and his death after two years (in 858).

¹⁰ Þintanceastre : according to the Annals of St Neots (Stevenson
213), Æþelwulf was first interred at Steyning ; cf F. M. Stenton,
Essays presented to T. F. Tout (1925), 17.

¹¹ On the genealogy of Æþelwulf cf Stevenson 157 ff, R. W.
Chambers, An Introduction to Beowulf (2d ed. Cambridge 1932),
195–204, 311–22. Beyond Cerdic, the earliest West Saxon king
mentioned here, we probably have some continental kings, but it is
difficult to say where history merges into myth in this line. Freapininʒ (l. 22) is probably a mistake for Frealafinʒ.

Enoh, Iaered, Maleel, Camon, Enos, Sed, Adam
primus homo et pater noster est Christus, Amen.
Ond þa fenȝon Æþelpulfes suna tpeȝen to rice,   30
Æþelbald to Þesseaxna rice 7 Æþelbryht to Cant-
para rice 7 to East-Seaxna rice 7 to Suþriȝea 7 to
Suþ-Seaxna rice ; 7 þa ricsode Æþelbald u ȝear.

Anno dccclx.   Her Æþelbald cynȝ forþferde 7 his lic liþ
æt Sciraburnan, 7 fenȝ Æþelbryht to allum þam rice
his broþur 7 he hit heold on ȝodre ȝeþuærnesse 7
on micelre sibsumnesse.   7 on his dæȝe cuom micel
sciphere up 7 abrecon Þintanceastre 7 piþ þone   5
here ȝefuhton Osric aldorman mid Hamtunscire 7
Æþelpulf aldormon mid Bearrucscire, 7 þone here
ȝefliemdon 7 pelstope ȝepald ahton.   7 se Æþelbryht
ricsode u ȝear 7 his lic liþ æt Scireburnan.

Anno dccclxu.   Her sæt heþen here on Tenet 7 ȝenamon
friþ piþ Cantparum, 7 Cantpare him feoh ȝeheton
piþ þam friþe, 7 under þam friþe 7 þam feohȝehate
se here hiene on niht up bestel, 7 oferherȝeade
alle Cent eastepearde.   5

855[30]. *Ond*, MS *O'*.

860. Below 860 in the margin is *añ dccclxi* opposite the second
line of the annal 860. 860[4]. *micelre*, MS *micelne*. 860[4]. *micel*
begins fol. 13b. 860[5]. The words *up.... pintancst'* are added
above the line to replace some deleted on this line (7 *only discern-
ible*) ; some have been deleted above the line after *pintancst'* (7
piδ......).   In the margin opposite the last three lines of this
annal are the year numbers 862, 863, 864.

---

[33] *þa ricsode Æþelbald u ȝear :* he died in 860.   His reign would
therefore begin in 856, probably on his father's return from Rome ;
according to the Annals of St Neots (Stevenson 132) he reigned two
and a half years with his father.

860[2]. *Sciraburnan*, Sherborne (Dorset), the seat of one of the
West Saxon bishoprics.

[9] *ricsode u ȝear :* as he became king in 860, he probably died
towards the end of the summer or in the early autumn of 865, for
his brother Æþered's succession is not recorded till 866 (which would
start, for the chronicler, in September 865).

865[1]. *ȝenamon friþ . . . up bestel :* Plummer II. cvii compares
Orosius (ed. H. Sweet, EETS lxxix, 218) : *he genom friþ wiþ þæt
folc 7 hiene siþþan aweg bestæl.*   Cf Introd. p. 7.

[3] *feohȝehate :* the first promise of Danegeld for the purchase of peace.

Anno dccclxui. Her fenჳ Æþered Æþelbryhtes broþur to
Þesseaxna rice ; 7 þy ilcan ჳeare cuom micel here
on Anჳelcynnes lond 7 pintersetl namon on East-
Enჳlum 7 þær ჳehorsude purdon 7 hie piþ him friþ
namon.   5

Anno dccclxuii. Her fór se here of East-Enჳlum ofer
Humbre muþan to Eoforpicceastre on Norþhymbre,
7 þær þæs micel unჳeþuærnes þære þeode betpeox
him selfum, 7 hie hæfdun hiera cyninჳ aporpenne
Osbryht 7 unჳecyndne cyninჳ underfenჳon Ællan ;   5

866⁴. piþ not in MS.

866². *cuom micel here :* this Danish army was led by the sons of
Ragnar Lothbrok, the famous Viking. From different sources it
appears that these were *Hinguar* (MS F 870, &c = ON *Ivarr inn Bein-
lausi* ' the boneless '), *Ubba* (ib. = ODan *Ubbo* in Saxo Grammati-
cus), *Healfdene* (875–7 *infra*, unknown in Scand. story) ; see also
878 notes. On these vikings cf A. Mawer, *Saga-book of the Viking
Society*, vi (1909), 68 ff. The army, which must have come in the
autumn of 865 (cf 867 note), remained in England and eventually
settled in Northumbria (876), Mercia (877) and East Anglia (880).

⁴ *ჳehorsude purdon :* On the Danish adoption of horses for speed
and mobility in traversing the country cf J. H. Clapham, EHR xxv.
287 ; cf also 894, 896, &c below.

867³. *micel unჳeþuærnes :* little is known of these dissensions in
Northumbria. Ella, the low-born usurper (863–7), had according
to *Ragnar Lothbrok's Saga* caused the death of Ragnar by casting
him into a snake pit and it was to avenge this that his sons came
to Northumbria. The fall of York was a serious blow to the English,
for it remained a Scandinavian possession for many generations.
The fight at York took place on the Friday before Palm Sunday
(21 March) 867 (Symeon of Durham, *Historiæ Recapitulatio*, Surtees
Society 51, p. 70) ; as the preceding union of Ella and Osbryht was
already *late on ჳeare*, the movement of the Danes to Northumbria
must be placed in the autumn of 866 (Beaven 338, cf Introd. p. 11) ;
this would involve putting the wintering in East Anglia (recorded
in 866) back to the autumn of 865.

⁶ *hie :* probably Osbryht and Ælla. Cf Symeon of Durham,
Historia Regum (Surtees Society 51), 48 : *discordia illa sedata est ;
rex vero Osbryht et Alla, adunatis viribus, congregatoque exercitu,
Eboracum adeunt opidum.*

⁷ *pinnende pærun :* the force of the participle is perhaps progressive and conditional, ' they resolved upon this, that they would
continue fighting the marauding army '.

7 hie late on ȝeare to þam ȝecirdon, þæt hie piþ
þone here pinnende pærun, 7 hie þeah micle fierd
ȝeȝadrodon 7 þone here sohton æt Eoforpicceastre
7 on þa ceastre brecon 7 hie sume inne purdon;
7 þær pas unȝemetlic pel ȝeslæȝen Norþanhymbra, 10
sume binnan, sume butan, 7 þa cyninȝas beȝen
ofslæȝene, 7 sio laf piþ þone here friþ nam. 7 þy
ilcan ȝeare ȝefór Ealchstan biscep 7 he hæfde þæt
bisceprice l pintra æt Scireburnan, 7 his lic liþ
þær on tune.   15

Anno dccclxuiii. Her fór se ilca here innan Mierce to
Snotenȝaham 7 þær pintersetl namon. 7 Burȝred
Miercna cyninȝ 7 his piotan bedon Æþered Pest-
Seaxna cyninȝ 7 Ælfred his broþur þæt hie him
ȝefultumadon, þæt hie piþ þone here ȝefuhton; 5
7 þa ferdon hie mid Pesseaxna fierde innan Mierce
oþ Snotenȝaham 7 þone here þær metton on þam
ȝepeorce, 7 þær nan hefelic ȝefeoht ne pearþ, 7
Mierce friþ namon piþ þone here.

Anno dccclxix. Her for se here eft to Eoforpicceastre
7 þær sæt i ȝear.

Anno dccclxx. Her rad se here ofer Mierce innan East-
Enȝle 7 pintersetl namon æt Þeodforda. 7 þy pintre

868. A cross in the margin opposite Ælfred's name.
870. 7 æþered . . . cantuareberi added by a later scribe.

---

[10] 7 þær pas unȝemetlic . . . : Plummer II. cvii compares Orosius :
þær wæs ungemetlic wæl geslagen. Cf Introd. p. 7.

[15] on tune, probably ' in the church-yard '; the original meaning
of tun was ' enclosure ' (A. Mawer, Chief Elements in English Place-
Names, EPN I. ii, 61), as in lic-tun ' burial ground ', cyric-tun
' church yard '. On the sense ' enclosure ' cf OE ontynan.

868. The movement of the Danes into winter-quarters at Nottingham was probably in the late autumn of 867 ; it would hardly have
been possible for all the events in this annal to have happened
between the autumn of 868 and the end of 868, even assuming that
the annalist's year began at Christmas ; cf Beaven 336.

870. The Danes moved to Thetford (Norfolk) in the autumn of
869, and Eadmund, therefore, was slain ' in that winter ' of 869–70 ;
Eadmund's death (20 November, according to Abbo of Fleury's
Passio Sancti Eadmundi) could hardly have been in November 870,

Eadmund cyninʒ him piþ feaht 7 þa Deniscan
siʒe namon 7 þone cyninʒ ofsloʒon 7 þæt lond all
ʒeeodon. 7 þy ʒeare ʒefór Ceolnoþ ærcebiscep;
7 Æþered Piltunscire biscop pearþ ʒecoren to ærce-
biscpe to Cantuareberi.

Anno dccclxxi. Her cuom se here to Readinʒum on
Pest-Seaxe, 7 þæs ymb iii niht ridon ii eorlas up.
Þa ʒemette hie Æþelpulf aldorman on Enʒlafelda,
7 him þær piþ ʒefeaht 7 siʒe nam. Þæs ymb iiii
niht Æþered cyninʒ 7 Ælfred his broþur þær micle
fierd to Readinʒum ʒeleddon 7 piþ þone here

871[7]. -fuhton begins fol. 14a.

---

for that would imply that East Anglia had been subdued and the
Danes had moved into Wessex between 20 November 870 and the
end of December 870 (cf 871 note and Beaven 336–7).

[3] *Eadmund cyninʒ :* St Eadmund, whose martyrdom is related
in Abbo of Fleury's *Passio Sancti Eadmundi*, followed by Ælfric
in his life of the saint ; cf G. Loomis, *The Growth of the St Edmund
Legend*, Harvard Studies in Philology and Literature, xiv (1932),
83–113, and *St Edmund and the Lodbrok legend* (ib. xv, 1933). Eadmund declined to become the vassal king of the pagan, Inguar ;
he was therefore bound to a tree, scourged and shot dead with
arrows.

[5] *Ceolnoþ*, archbishop of Canterbury, died 4 February 870 (MS
D adds *to Rome*).

871. Bishop Heahmund (see l. 28) died 22 March (the date of his
obit in the English Calendar) ; from this date the dates of certain
battles can be approximately determined (cf Beaven 334–5) :
Reading 28 December 870, Englefield 31 December 870, Reading
4 January 871, Ashdown 8 January, Basing 22 January, and, of
course, *Meretune* 22 March 871, when Heahmund was slain. The
remaining events would be Easter 15 April 871, Æþered's death
'after Easter' (possibly the second fortnight of April 871), Ælfred
at Wilton by the end of May 871. As the first event in this annal
is dated 28 December 870, it is usually supposed (Plummer, *Life
and Times of Alfred*, 93, Hoffmann-Hirtz 74n) that the annalist
changed his year at Christmas 870, but since the Chronicle records
no events between 4 February 870 (see 870[5]n) and 28 December 870,
there is nothing to shew that he was not following his usual practice
of changing his year in September.

[2] *eorlas*, the OE adaptation of ON *jarl*, equivalent as a designation
of rank to OE *aldormon* (cf H. M. Chadwick, *Anglo-Saxon Institutions*, 1905, p. 382).

ʒefuhton, 7 þær þæs micel wæl ʒeslæʒen on ʒe-
hƿæþre hond, 7 Æþelƿulf aldormon þearþ ofslæʒen,
7 þa Deniscan ahton ƿælstoƿe ʒeƿald. 7 þæs
ymb iiii niht ʒefeaht Æþered cyninʒ 7 Ælfred his 10
broþur þiþ alne þone here on Æscesdune, 7 hie
þærun on tƿæm ʒefylcum ; on oþrum þæs Bachsecʒ 7 Halfdene þa hæþnan cyninʒas, 7 on oþrum
þæron þa eorlas. 7 þa ʒefeaht se cyninʒ Æþered
þiþ þara cyninʒa ʒetruman 7 þær þearþ se cyninʒ 15
Baʒsecʒ ofslæʒen, 7 Ælfred his broþur þiþ þara eorla
ʒetruman 7 þær þearþ Sidroc eorl ofslæʒen se alda,
7 Sidroc eorl se ʒioncʒa, 7 Osbearn eorl 7 Fræna eorl
7 Hareld eorl ; 7 þa herʒas beʒen ʒefliemde 7 fela
þusenda ofslæʒenra 7 on feohtende þæron oþ niht. 20
7 þæs ymb xiiii niht ʒefeaht Æþered cyninʒ 7 Ælfred
his broður þiþ þone here æt Basenʒum 7 þær þa
Deniscan siʒe namon. 7 þæs ymb ii monaþ ʒefeaht
Æþered cyninʒ 7 Ælfred his broþur þiþ þone here
æt Meretune, 7 hie þærun on tuæm ʒefylcium 7 hie 25

871[11]. A cross in margin, and a small one over *on*.

---

[11] *on Æscesdune* : the name survives in Ashdown Park in Ash-
bury (Berkshire), but it referred in OE times to a great tract of the
Berkshire Downs (Mawer 44).

[12] *Bachsecʒ* : the names of the Danish leaders here and elsewhere
are discussed by E. Björkman, *Nordische Personennamen in England*
and *Zur englischen Namenkunde* (Halle, 1910, 1912) and J. Jónsson,
Vikingasaga um Herferðir Vikinga (Reykjavik 1915), 103 ; *Bachsecʒ* = ON *Bakskiki* (?), *Halfdene* (cf 862[2]n) = ODan *Halfdanr*,
Sidroc = ON *Sigtryggr* (?), *Osbearn* = ON *Ásbjǫrn*, *Fræna* = ON
Fræni, *Hareld* = ON *Haraldr*. Only Halfdene can be identified.

[19] *ʒefliemde*, p.pt. after *þæron* (l. 20).

[25] *æt Meretune* (so MS C ; *Merantune* B, *Meredune* D, *Mæredune*
E) ; whichever form is correct identification is uncertain, for *Meretune* is a very common OE place-name, whilst a proposed equation
of *Mæredune* with Marden (Wiltshire) is improbable, as that name
is from OE *denu* (cf Mawer 49–50).

[25] *hie þærun on tuæm ʒefylcium . . . :* it is not clear whether the
English or the Danes were in two divisions ; cf G. Rübens, *Parataxe
und Hypotaxe* (1915), 18. A possible parallel is found in l. 12 above,
where the next sentence makes it clear that the Danes are meant.
If that is so here, then the English success was only temporary
(cf 837[5]n). *ʒefylce* is probably a loan from ON *fylki*.

27

butu ʒefliemdon 7 lonʒe on dæʒ siʒe ahton, 7 þær
pearþ micel pelsliht on ʒehpeþere hond 7 þa Deniscan
ahton pelstope ʒepald ; 7 þær pearþ Heahmund
biscep ofslæʒen 7 fela ʒodra monna ; 7 æfter þissum
ʒefeohte cuom micel sumorlida. 7 þæs ofer Eastron ³⁰
ʒefor Æþered cyninʒ, 7 he ricsode u ʒear, 7 his lic liþ
æt Pinburnam.

Þa fenʒ Ælfred Æþelpulfinʒ his broþur to Pesseaxna rice, 7 þæs ymb anne monaþ ʒefeaht Ælfred
cyninʒ piþ alne þone here lytle perede æt Piltune, ³⁵
7 hine lonʒe on dæʒ ʒefliemde, 7 þa Deniscan ahton
pelstope ʒepald. 7 þæs ʒeares purdon uiiii folcʒe-
feoht ʒefohten piþ þone here on þy cynerice be suþan
Temese, butan þam þe him Ælfred þæs cyninʒes
broþur 7 anlipiʒ aldormon 7 cyninʒes þeʒnas oft ⁴⁰
rade on ridon þe mon na ne rimde ; 7 þæs ʒeares
pærun ofslæʒene uiiii eorlas 7 an cyninʒ. 7 þy
ʒeare namon Pest-Seaxe friþ piþ þone here.

Anno dccclxxii. Her fór se here to Lundenbyriʒ from

871³³. A cross in margin. 871³⁹. *butan*, MS 7 *butan*. 871⁴¹. *mon
na*, MS *monna*, with a stroke under the first *n* to separate the words.

---

³⁰ *sumorlida*, ON *sumarliði* ' summer army ', possibly with a base in
Flanders (cf Hoffmann-Hirtz 76n2) ; Ethelwerd (*Monumenta Hist.
Brit.*, 1848, 514) has : *advenit sine numero æstivus exercitus.*

³⁵ *lytle perede :* instr. used as dative of accompaniment.

³⁷ *7 þæs ʒeares . . . onridon :* Plummer II. cvii suggests a parallel
in Orosius (*ed. cit.* 118) : *he leng mid folcgefeohtum wið hie ne mehte,
ac oftrædlice he wæs mid hloþum on hi hergende* (cf. Introd. p. 7).

³⁹ *butan þam þe . . . ne rimde :* ' excluding those innumerable
raids which Ælfred the king's brother and an individual alderman
. . . rode on.' For *anlipiʒ aldermon*, Asser has *singuli duces illius
gentis cum suis,* but other versions have simply *ealdormen* ; *anlipiʒ*
means ' going alone, solitary ' ; *aldermon* should perhaps be emended
aldormen.

⁴⁰ *cyninʒes þeʒnas :* a *þeʒn* was a personal servant and but one
degree higher in the ranks of freemen than a *ceorl* (the lowest), but
as servants of the king the status of *þeʒn* rose, until they formed the
elected nobility of the kingdom (cf H. M. Chadwick, *Anglo-Saxon
Institutions,* 77–87, 309–11, 327).

872. The movement to London was probably in the autumn of
871, for it is unlikely that the Danes would have remained at
Reading from the summer of 871 until the autumn of 872.

Readinȝum 7 þæʳ pintersetl nam, 7 þa namon **Mierce**
friþ piþ þone here.

Anno dccclxxiii.   Her for se here on Norþhymbre 7 he nam
pintersetl on Lindesse æt Turecesieȝe, 7 þa namon
Mierce friþ piþ þone here.

Anno dccclxxiiii.   Her for se here from Lindesse to
Hreopedune 7 þær pintersetl nam, 7 þone cyninȝ
Burȝrᴇd ofer sᴇ adræfdon ymb xxii pintra þæs þe
he rice hæfde 7 þæt lond all ȝeeodon ; 7 he fór
to Rome 7 þær ȝesæt 7 his lic liþ on Sancta Marian   **5**
ciricean on Anȝelcynnes scole.   7 þy ilcan ȝeare hie
sealdon anum unpisum cyninȝes þeȝne Miercna rice
to haldanne 7 he him aþas spor 7 ȝislas salde þæt
he him ȝearo pære spa hpelce dæȝe spa hie hit habban
polden 7 he ȝearo pære mid him selfum 7 on allum   **10**
þam þe him læstan poldon to þæs heres þearfe.

Anno dccclxxu.   Her for se here from Hreopedune 7
Healfdene fór mid sumum þam here on Norþhymbre
7 nam pintersetl be Tinan þære ei 7 se here þæt
lond ȝeeode 7 oft herȝade on Peohtas 7 on Strᴇcled-
Þalas.   7 for Ȝodrum 7 Oscytel 7 Anpynd, þa iii   **5**
cyninȝas, of Hreopedune to Ȝrantebrycȝe mid
micle here 7 sæton þær an ȝear.   7 þy sumera for

---

873. *Lindesse æt*, MS *lindesseæt*, with a stroke under the second *e*
to separate the words.

874⁵. *-sæt 7 his lic* begins fol. 14b.

875⁴. *oft*, MS *eft*, *e* dotted and *o* added above.

---

874. The wintering at Repton probably belongs to the October
of 873 (cf Beaven 336).

⁶ *Anȝelcynnes scole :* a hostel for English pilgrims ; cf Plummer
II. 69, Stevenson 243–7.

875. The wintering on the Tyne and at Cambridge probably
began in the autumn of 874 and precedes the summer naval battle
(l. 8).

² *Healfdene*, the brother of Inpær (cf 878⁷) and a son of Ragnar
Lothbrok (cf 866²n) ; nothing is known of Halfdene in Scandinavian
sources.   He encamped at the mouth of the Team near Newcastle
(Symeon of Durham), and his depredations, or the fear of them,
drove the monks of Lindisfarne away with their treasures—the body
of St Cuthbert and the Lindisfarne Gospels (cf Plummer II. 89–90).

Ælfred cyninȝ ut on sǽ mid sciphere 7 ȝefeaht piþ
uii sciphlæstas, 7 hiera an ȝefenȝ 7 þa oþru ȝefliemde. 10

Anno dccclxxui. Her hiene bestǽl se here into Þerham
Þesseaxna fierde 7 piþ þone here se cyninȝ friþ nam
7 him þa aþas sporon on þam halȝan beaȝe, þe
hie ær nanre þeode noldon, þæt hie hrǽdlice of his
rice foren ; 7 hie þa under þam hie nihtes bestǽlon 5
þære fierde, se ȝehorsoda here, into Escanceaster.
7 þy ȝeare Healfdene Norþanhymbra lond ȝedǽlde
7 erȝende pæron 7 hiera tilȝende.

Anno dccclxxuii. Her cuom se here into Escanceastre
from Þerham, 7 se sciphere siȝelede pest ymbutan,
7 þa mette hie micel yst on sǽ, 7 þær forpearþ cxx
scipa æt Spanapic. 7 se cyninȝ Ælfred æfter
þam ȝehorsudan here mid fierde rád oþ Exanceaster 5
7 hie hindan ofridan ne meahte ær hie on þam
fæstene pæron, þær him mon to ne meahte ; 7 hie
him þær foreȝislas saldon, spa fela spa he habban
polde, 7 micle aþas sporon, 7 þa ȝodne friþ heoldon.
7 þa on hærfeste ȝefor se here on Miercna lond 7 hit 10
ȝedǽldon sum 7 sum Ceolpulfe saldon.

876². *Þesseaxna fierde*, gen. after *hiene* (reflex. pron.) *bestǽl*,
' away from, eluding the army of the West Saxons '. This *here* is
that from Cambridge.

³ *on þam halȝan beaȝe*, the sacred ring, which was kept in the
heathen temple and over which oaths were sworn ; most allusions
to the sacred ring are in Scandinavian sources (cf R. Cleasby and
G. Vigfusson, *Icelandic Dictionary*, s.v. *baugr*, *baug-eiðr*, *stalla-
hringr*, Plummer II. 90, and J. Hoops, *Reallexikon*, s.v. *Eid*).

⁶ *se ȝehorsoda here*, in apposition to *hie* (l. 5) ; the second *hie*
is reflexive to *bestǽlon*.

⁷ *Norþanhymbra lond ȝedǽlde* : the first recorded settlement of
Danes in England. The settlement was confined to Yorkshire,
especially the Vale of York (cf *Place-Names of the North Riding*
(EPN V), xxi).

⁸ *hiera tilȝende* : *hiera* is gen. reflexive pronoun, ' continued to
make a living for themselves '.

877¹⁰ *on hærfeste* : the OE *hærfest* began 7 August. The movement to Mercia, therefore, fell between 7 August and the end of
the year (i.e. 23 September, cf. Introd. p. 11).

¹¹ *Ceolpulf* : cf 874⁷, *anum unpisum cyninȝes þeȝne*.

Anno dccclxxuiii. Her hiene bestᵉl se here on midne
pinter ofer tuelftan niht to Cippanhamme 7 ȝeridon
Þesseaxna lond 7 ȝesæton 7 micel þæs folces ofer sᵉ
adræfdon 7 þæs oþres þone mæstan dᵉl hie ȝeridon
7 him to ȝecirdon buton þam cyninȝe Ælfrede, 7 he   5
lytle perede unieþelice æfter þudum for 7 on mor-
fæstenum. 7 þæs ilcan pintra þæs Inpæres broþur
7 Healfdenes on Þest-Seaxum on Defenascire mid
xxiii scipum 7 hiene mon þær ofsloȝ 7 dccc monna
mid him 7 xl monna his heres. 7 þæs on Eastron   10
þorhte Ælfred cyninȝ lytle perede ȝepeorc æt Æþelinȝaeiȝȝe 7 of þam ȝepeorce þas þinnende þiþ
þone here 7 Sumursætna se dᵉl se þær niehst þæs.
Þa on þære seofoðan þiecan ofer Eastron he ȝerad

878³. 7 micel þæs folces ofer, MS micel þæs folces 7 ofer. 878⁷.
broþur begins fol. 15a.

878¹. on midne pinter . . . : ' about mid-winter ' (i.e. 25 Decem-
ber) or ' in the middle of winter after Twelfth Night ' (7 January).
This treacherous move by the Danes at an unusual season took
Wessex by surprise.

³ 7 micel þæs folces ofer sᵉ : so all MSS but A, where the ampersand
is misplaced before folces.

⁷ Inpæres broþur 7 Healfdenes : Gaimar says that this was Ubba
(see above 866²n) and that he was buried in a great mound called
Ubbelawe, which zealous antiquarians have identified with a lost
Ubbaston or Whibbleston near Appledore ; this is discountenanced
by Stevenson 263. All other MSS of the Chronicle state that at
the battle in Devonshire the Danes lost ' the standard which they
called the Raven ', and an interpolation in Asser adds that ' this
had been woven in one day by the three daughters of (Ragnar)
Lothbrok ' (Stevenson 44).

¹⁰ 7 xl monna his heres : heres (in all MSS) is perhaps a mistake
for hiredes ' retinue ' (ex inf. Professor Dickins).

¹⁰ on Eastron : 23 March 878. From this the remaining events
of this annal can be approximately dated : Ecȝbryhtesstan about
11 May ; Iley about 12 May ; Eddington about 13 May ; þæt
ȝepeorc from about 13 May to 27 May ; Aller about 17 June ;
crismlisinȝ at Wedmore about 24 June ; Guthorm remaining with
the king to about 29 June or 6 July according to whether the 12 days
dates from his baptism or crismlisinȝ.

¹¹ æt Æþelinȝaeiȝȝe : Athelney was at the confluence of the
R. Parrett and the R. Tone.

to Ecȝbryhtesstane be eastan Sealpyda 7 him to ¹
comon þær onȝen Sumorsæte alle 7 Þilsætan 7
Hamtunscir se dęl se hiere behinon sę pas 7 his
ȝefæȝene pærun. 7 he fór ymb ane niht of þam
picum to Iȝlea 7 þæs ymb ane to Eþandune 7 þær
ȝefeaht piþ alne þone here 7 hiene ȝefliemde 7 him ²
æfter rád oþ þæt ȝepeorc 7 þær sæt xiiii niht ; 7 þa
salde se here him foreȝislas 7 micle aþas, þæt hie
of his rice uuoldon, 7 him eac ȝeheton þæt hiera
kyninȝ fulpihte onfon polde 7 hie þæt ȝelæston

878¹⁶. comon, MS có, mon added by later hand above line.

---

¹⁵ Ecȝbryhtesstane : the name, as well as the site, is lost, probably
beyond recovery (cf Mawer 48, Stevenson 268), though attempts
have been made to locate it, quite reasonably, near Penzelwood by
Selwood Forest on the borders of Wiltshire, Somerset and Dorset
(cf A. F. Major, Early Wars of Wessex, 1913, 171).

¹⁷ se dęl se hiere behinon sę pas, ' that part of it (Hampshire)
which was on this side of the sea '. R. W. Chambers, England
before the Norman Conquest (1926), 210 note, takes sę to be Southampton Water and the part of Hampshire to be West Hampshire ;
the Chronicler would then be writing in the south-west and not at
Winchester (cf Introd. p. 9). But until the sę can be identified,
any interpretation must remain doubtful. Even if Southampton
Water is meant there is no evidence which part of Hampshire is the
excluded portion ; the choice of West Hampshire rests upon the
suggestion that the Chronicle is south-western in origin. A better
interpretation is suggested by Asser : ibique obviaverunt illi omnes
accolae Summurtunensis pagae et Wiltunensis, omnes accolae Ham-
tunensis qui non ultra mare pro metu paganorum navigaverunt.
The Chronicle might therefore refer to those men of Hampshire who
had not fled beyond the sea from the Danes ; cf l. 3 above.

¹⁹ Iȝlea, (MS E Æȝlea), a lost Iley Oak, near Warminster (Stevenson 272, Mawer 49).

²¹ þæt ȝepeorc : this may be Chippenham, the Danish centre for
this campaign (cf l. 2 above).

²² salde se here him foreȝislas : the so-called Treaty of Wedmore ; Wedmore (l. 29), however, was only the scene of Guthrum's
crismlisinȝ.

²⁴ fulpihte onfon : on the adoption of Christianity by the Danes
cf W. G. Collingwood, Antiquity i. 172–180. There was no real
adoption of faith, but the observance of Christian ceremonies was a
matter of convenience to them. This use of onfon (also at 893⁵⁵)
is perhaps due to Latin suscipere.

spa. 7 þæs ymb iii piecan com se cyninȝ to him [25]
ȝodrum þritiȝa sum þara monna, þe in þam here
peorþuste pæron, æt Alre, 7 þæt is piþ Æþel-
inȝȝaeiȝe ; 7 his se cyninȝ þær onfenȝ æt fulpihte
7 his crismlisinȝ pas æt Þeþmor 7 he pas xii niht
mid þam cyninȝe 7 he hine miclum 7 his ȝeferan [30]
mid feo peorðude.

Anno dccclxxix.   Her for se here to Cirenceastre of Cippanhamme 7 sæt þær án ȝear, 7 þy ȝeare ȝeȝadrode
an hloþ picenȝa 7 ȝesæt æt Fullanhamme be Temese.
7 þy ilcan ȝeare aþiestrode sio sunne ane tid dæȝes.

Anno dccclxxx.   Her for se here of Cirenceastre on East-
Enȝle 7 ȝesæt þæt lond 7 ȝedẹlde.   7 þy ilcan ȝeare
fór se here ofer sẹ, þe ær on Fullanhomme sæt, on
Fronclond to ȝend, 7 sæt þær an ȝear.

Anno dccclxxxi.   Her for se here ufor on Fronclond 7 þa

878[27]. *peorþuste*, MS *peorþȝte*.   879[3]. *an hloþ*, MS *on hloþ*.

---

[29] *crismlisinȝ*, the removal after 8 days of the white cloth (the
chrismale) bound round the head at baptism to keep the unction
on the head during the week the baptized person wore white robes
wherein he appeared daily at church with his sponsors (cf C. Plummer, *Bede's Hist. Eccles.* II. 280).

879. The events of this annal probably took place in the autumn
of 878 ; the army which had made peace with Ælfred at the end of
the 878 campaign and which had sworn oaths *þæt hie of his rice
uuoldon* (878[22]) is unlikely to have remained at Chippenham, their
headquarters (cf 878[2], 878[21]n), until 879 ; their move to Cirencester
must have fallen in the autumn of 878 (cf Beaven 339).   The eclipse
fell on 29 October 878 (Stevenson 280–6) ; this eclipse is perhaps
referred to again in a charter of Ælfred's (W. de G. Birch, *Cartu-
larium Saxonicum*, 549, 1 November 878), dated ' 979 (sic for 879),
*indictione xiiii, kal' November, in hunc annum sol obscuratum fuit '.
Plummer (II. 95), assuming a Christmas beginning for the year,
supposed that this annal was one year out, the error persisting till
897, that is, actually 896 (but cf Introd. p. 11).

[2] *ȝeȝadrode an hloþ picenȝa* : Plummer II. cvii compares Orosius
(*ed. cit.* 116) : *he scipa gegaderode 7 wicengas wurdon*.   Cf. Introd. p. 7.

880. The army went to Ghent in November 879 (*Annales
Vedastini*, ed. B. de Simson (Hannover 1900), 45, Beaven 331).   The
move to East Anglia probably also belongs to the late autumn of 879.

881. The fight against the Franks was the Battle of Saucourt (in
which the Franks were the victors) fought in August 881 (*Annales*

Francan him piþ ȝefuhton 7 þær þa pearþ se here
ȝehorsod æfter þam ȝefeohte.

Anno dccclxxxii. Her for se here up onlonȝ Mæse feor
on Fronclond 7 þær sæt an ȝear. 7 þy ilcan ȝeare
fór Ælfred cyninȝ mid scipum ut on sæ 7 ȝefeaht
piþ feoper sciphlæstas Deniscra monna 7 þara scipa
tu ȝenam, 7 þa men ofslæȝene pæron þe ðæron ⁵
pæron, 7 tueȝen scipheras him on hond eodon 7
þa pæron miclum forslæȝene 7 forþundode ær hie
on hond eodon.

Anno dccclxxxiii. Her for se here up on Scald to Cundoþ
7 þær sæt an ȝear.

Anno dccclxxxiiii. Her for se here up on Sunnan to
Embenum 7 þær sæt án ȝear.

Anno dccclxxxu. Her todælde se foresprecena here on tu,
oþer dæl east, oþer dæl to Hrofesceastre, 7 ymbsæton
ða ceastre 7 þorhton oþer fæsten ymb hie selfe,

Fuldenses, ed. F. Kurze (Hannover 1891), 96, Beaven 332); this
battle is the subject of the Old High German Ludwigslied (W.
Braune, Althochdeutsches Lesebuch, 1928, no. xxxvi). The Annales
Fuldenses also refer to the Norsemen increasing the number of their
equites. Plummer who assumed that these entries in the Chronicle
were one year out (cf 879n above) proposed an earlier fight in 880,
but an event which happened in August 881 (i.e. before September 24) would rightly be entered under 881 ; the allusion to the
horsing of the Danes in both the Chronicle and the Annales Fuldenses
is also significant.

882. Soon after the Battle of Saucourt (see 881n), the Danes
moved up the Meuse in November 881 (Beaven 331-2), which
falls within the annalistic year 882 ; the annalist changed his
year between these two events (cf Introd. p. 11).

883. The move up the Scheldt to Conde took place in October
882 (Annales Vedastini, ed. cit. 52).

884. The Danes moved to Amiens on the Somme in October 883
(Annales Vedastini, ed. cit. 54).

885. This annal deals first with English events, the siege of
Rochester possibly beginning in November 884, for according to
the Annales Vedastini (ed. cit. 55) the Danes left Amiens at the end
of October 884, some crossing the sea, the rest going to Louvain
(cf Beaven 333). Ælfred raised the siege and the Danes withdrew
over the sea in the same summer (i.e. the summer of 885) ; the two
fights at the mouth of the Stour perhaps also belong to this summer.

7 hie þeah þa ceastre aperedon oþþæt Ælfred com
utan mid fierde. Þa eode se here to hiera scipum   5
7 forlet þæt ʒepeorc, 7 hie purdon þær behorsude,
7 sona þy ilcan sumere ofer sǫ ʒepiton. 7 þy
ilcan ʒeare sende Aelfred cyninʒ sciphere on East-
Enʒle. Sona spa hie comon on Sture muþan,
þa metton hie xui scipu picenʒa 7 piþ ða ʒefuhton,   10
7 þa scipo alle ʒerǫhton 7 þa men ofsloʒon. Þa hie
þa hampeard pendon mid þære herehyþe, þa
metton hie micelne sciphere picenʒa 7 þa piþ þa
ʒefuhton þy ilcan dæʒe, 7 þa Deniscan ahton siʒe.
þy ilcan ʒeare ær middum pintra forþferde Carl   15
Francna cyninʒ 7 hiene ofsloʒ án efor, 7 ane
ʒeare ær his broður forþferde, se hæfde eac þæt
pestrice, 7 hie pæron beʒen Hloþpiʒes suna, se
hæfde eac þæt pestrice 7 forþferde þy ʒeare þe
sio sunne aþiestrode ; se pæs Karles sunu þe Æþel-   20

885[4]. *aperedon, o* might be read as *e*. *cô utan* begins fol. 15b ;
utan above the line. 885[8]. *Aelfred*, so MS. 885[9]. *Sture*, MS *stufe*.
885[16]. *ofsloʒ án*, MS *ofsloʒán*, with a stroke under ʒ to separate
the words.

[9] *on Sture muþan :* MSS A[1], A[2], B, C and Ethelwerd read *Stufe*
corrected to *Sture* in A[2] against *Sture* in the rest.

[10] *þa metton hie xui scipu :* Thorpe takes *hie* as acc. but it is pref-
erably the subject of *metton* ; cf also for the word-order the unam-
biguous sentence *þa metton hie micelne sciphere* (l. 15).

[15] Of the continental events the following can be dated (cf Beaven
333–4) : death of Carloman 12 December 884 ; death of Louis the
Stammerer (l. 19) 10 April 879 in the year of the eclipse 29 October
878 (see 879n) ; the two Danish attacks on the Old Saxons (l. 23),
one at Norden in Frisia about December 884 (cf Stevenson 292),
the other in Saxony (where the Frisians attacked the Danes from
behind) about May 885 ; the accession of Charles the Fat (l. 25)
not before June 885 ; the death of Pope Marinus (l. 33) probably
15 May 884. With the exception of the last, all these dates are
consistent with a year beginning in September.

[15] *middum pintra*, Mid-Winter (December 25) ; *Carl* = Carloman.

[17] *his broður :* Louis (died August 882), son of Louis the Stammerer.

[20] *se pæs Karles sunu :* Louis the Stammerer was the son of Charles
the Bald, whose daughter Judith had married Æþelwulf (see also
l. 29 and 855[2]n).

pulf Þest-Seaxna cyninʒ his dohtor hæfde him to
cuene. 7 þy ilcan ʒeare ʒeʒadrode micel sciphere
on Ald-Seaxum, 7 þær pearþ micel ʒefeoht, tua
on ʒeare, 7 þa Seaxan hæfdun siʒe, 7 þær
pæron Frisan mid. Þy ilcan ʒeare fenʒ Carl to [25]
þam þestrice 7 to allum þam þestrice behienan
Þendelsþ 7 beʒeondan þisse sþ spa hit his þridda
fþder hæfde, butan Lidpiccium; se Carl pas Hloþpiʒes sunu; se Hloþpiʒ pas Carles broþur, se pæs
Iuþyttan fþder þe Æþelpulf cyninʒ hæfde, 7 hie [30]
pæron Hloþpiʒes suna; se Hloþpiʒ pas þæs aldan
Carles sunu; se Carl pas Pippenes sunu. 7 þy
ilcan ʒeare forþferde se ʒoda papa Mar nus, se ʒe-
freode Onʒelcynnes scole be Ælfredes bene Þest-
Seaxna cyninʒes, 7 he sende him micla ʒifa 7 [35]
þære rode dþl þe Crist on þroþude. 7 þy ilcan
ʒeare se here on East-Enʒlum brþc friþ piþ Ælfred
cyninʒ.

[25] *Carl :* Charles the Fat, son of Louis the German (l. 28), who
was the brother of Charles the Bald (l. 29), both sons of Louis
the Pious (died 840), son of Charles the Great (ll. 31–2).

[27] *beʒeondan þisse sþ :* ' beyond this sea '; Plummer takes *þisse
sþ* to be *Þendelsþ*, i.e. the Mediterranean (Plummer II. 98), but G. P.
Krapp and A. G. Kennedy, *An Anglo-Saxon Reader* (New York
1929), 173, suggest that *þisse sþ* is the English Channel.

[27] *spa hit . . . hæfde :* Charles the Fat acquired Swabia and
Alsace in 876, Italy in 881, the eastern kingdom (Germany) on the
death of his brother Louis in 882, and the western kingdom in 885
after the death of Carloman in 884. This was in effect the empire
of his great-grandfather Charles the Great.

[28] *butan Lidpiccium* (MSS C, D, have *Lidpicinʒum*) ; Thorpe
II. 67 cites Florence of Worcester's translation of these words as
absque Armoricano regno and connects the name with *Llydaw*
(Latin *Letauia*), the Welsh name for Brittany. Brittany became
independent in 840.

[36] *þære rode dþl :* in some MSS the sending of a piece of the True
Cross is also recorded under 883. On the possible associations of
this fragment of the Cross with the Brussels Cross see B. Dickins
and A. S. C. Ross, *The Dream of the Rood*, 15.

[37] The breaking of the peace by the East Anglian Danes probably
followed upon the Danish victory at the mouth of the Stour (see
l. 10 above), and belongs therefore to the summer of 885.

Anno dccclxxxui. Her for se here eft ƿest þe ær east
ʒelende, 7 þa up on Siʒene 7 þær ƿintersetl namon.
Þy ilcan ʒeare ʒesette Ælfred cyninʒ Lundenburʒ,
7 him all Anʒelcyn to cirde, þæt buton Deniscra
monna hæftniede þas, 7 he þa befæste þa burʒ　　5
Æþerede aldormen to haldonne.
Anno dccclxxxuii. Her for se here up þurh þa brycʒe

886[5]. he, MS hie.

886[2] *up on Siʒene* : the Danes went up the Seine (to Paris in
MS E), in the autumn of 885, for the Siege of Paris lasted from
November 885 to November 886 (Beaven 332).

[3] *ʒesette . . . Lundenburʒ* : the recapture of London (cf 851
above) probably took place in the autumn of 885 and was the final
incident in the active campaign of 885 (see annal 885 and cf Beaven
341–2). It resulted in the Treaty of Ælfred and Guthrum which
defined the boundary between English and Danish territory as
' up the Lea to its source, then straight across to the Ouse at Bed-
ford, then along the Ouse to Watling Street and along Watling
Street ' (B. Thorpe, *Ancient Laws and Institutes*, 1840, I. 152).

[4] *þæt buton . . . :* ' except for that part of the English race which
was under the rule of the Danish men '.

[6] *Æþerede aldormen* : alderman of Mercia, husband of Ælfred's
daughter, Æþelflæd ' lady of the Mercians '.

887. Danish continental campaigns for two years are noted in
this annal. In autumn 886 the Norsemen went up the Seine from
Paris and entered the Yonne, encamping at Sens (*Annales Vedastini*,
ed. cit. 63). About May 887 they returned to Paris to collect tribute,
returned again by the Seine, entered the Marne and established a
camp at Chezy-sur-Marne (*Annales Vedastini* 63). The wintering
at Sens would normally be entered in the Chronicle under 887. The
encamping at Chezy may have happened in the summer or early
autumn of 887 (before 24 September), in which case it is rightly
entered under 887 ; but if it took place in the late autumn of 887
then it should have been entered under 888 and in this case its
premature entry under 887 may be compared with that of the
death of Charles the Fat (l. 4) which took place 13 January 888.
Plummer II. 101 suggests that *innan Ionan* refers to the Norsemen's move in the autumn of 888 by the Marne and the Seine to the
Loing (*Annales Vedastini* 67), an affluent of the Seine a little below
the Yonne ; he assumes that the order of the two encampments
oþ Cariei and *innan Ionan* as given in the Chronicle is correct, but
it was perhaps uncertainty as to their order that caused the events
of two years to be entered in one annal ; besides this, *innan Ionan*
must mean ' within the valley of the Yonne ', not ' below the Yonne '.

37

æt Paris 7 þa up andlanᵹ Siᵹene oþ Mæterne oþ
Cariei. 7 þa sæton þara 7 innan Ionan, tu þinter
on þam tþam stedum. 7 þy ilcan ᵹeare forþferde
Karl Francna cyninᵹ, 7 Earnulf his broþur sunu   5
hine ui picum ær he forþferde berᵹdde æt þam
rice, 7 þa pearþ þæt rice todᵹled on u 7 u kyninᵹas
to ᵹehalᵹode ; þæt pæs þeah mid Earnulfes ᵹeþaf-
unᵹe 7 hi cuᵹdon þæt hie þæt to his honda healdan
sceoldon, forþæm hira nán næs on fᵹdrenhealfe to   10
ᵹeboren buton him anum. Earnulf þa þunode
on þᵹm londe be eastan Rin 7 Roþulf þa fenᵹ to
þæm middelrice 7 Óda to þæm þestdᵹle 7 Beornᵹar
7 Þiþa to Lonᵹbeardna londe 7 to þæm londum on þa
healfe muntes, 7 þæt heoldun mid micelre unsibbe 15
7 tu folcᵹefeoht ᵹefuhton 7 þæt lond oft 7 ᵹelome
forherᵹodon, 7 æᵹhpᵹþer oþerne oft rᵹdlice ut
dræfde. 7 þy ilcan ᵹeare þe se here for forþ up
ofer þa brycᵹe æt Paris, Æþelhelm aldormon lᵹdde
Þesseaxna ᵹlmessan 7 Ælfredes cyninᵹes to Rome. 20
Anno dccclxxxuiii. Her lᵹdde Beocca aldormon Þesseaxna
ᵹlmessan 7 Ælfredes cyninᵹes to Rome ; 7 Æþel-

887⁶. berᵹdde, MS berᵹd ne.   887¹⁰. -healfe begins fol. 16a.
887¹⁹. Æþelhelm, MS 7 ᵹþelhelm.   887²⁰. 7 added above the line.
888. A large cross above the year number.

---

³ *Cariei* (A, B, C) : D, E, F read, perhaps correctly, *Caziei* ; cf
Annales Vedastini (*ed. cit.* 64) : *Dani . . . iterum per Sequanum
Maternam fluvium ingressi Gaziaco sibi castra statuunt.*

⁷ *todᵹled on u :* Arnulf took the eastern kingdom (Germany),
Rudolf the middle kingdom (Burgundy), Odo the western kingdom
(Aquitaine, &c), and Guido and Berengar Lombardy and Italy,
over which they fought two battles, Brescia in autumn 888 when
Berengar was victor, and Trebbia in spring 889, when Guido won the
victory. These two battles are prematurely recorded in the Chronicle.

¹⁰ *on fᵹdrenhealfe :* Arnulf only was connected with the male line
and he was a bastard son of Carloman.

²⁰ *Þesseaxna ᵹlmessan :* suggested to be Peter's Pence (cf Hoffmann-Hirtz 87n) ; Stevenson 211n.2 cites a letter from Pope
Alexander II to William the Conqueror which says that the English
used formerly to send a yearly sum to Rome, part for the pope, part
for the English school.

888². *Æþelspiþ cuen :* wife of Burᵹred, king of Mercia (cf 853¹³, 874).

spiþ cuen, sio pæs Ælfredes speostor cyninჳes,
forþferde, 7 hire lic liþ æt Pafian. 7 þy ilcan
ჳeare Æþelred ercebiscep 7 Æþelpold aldormon   5
forþferdon on anum monþe.

Anno dccclxxxuiiii. On þissum ჳeare næs nan fęreld to
Rome, buton tueჳen hleaperas Ælfred cyninჳ sende
mid ჳepritum.

Anno dcccxc. Her lędde Beornhelm abbud Þest-Seaxna
ęlmessan to Rome 7 Ælfredes cyninჳes. 7 Jodrum
se norþerna cyninჳ forþferde, þæs fulluht nama pæs
Æþelstan, se pæs Ælfredes cyninჳes ჳodsunu,
7 he bude on East-Enჳlum 7 þæt lond ærest ჳesæt.   5
7 þy ilcan ჳeare for se here of Siჳene to Sant Laudan
þæt is betueoh Brettum 7 Francum, 7 Brettas him
piþ ჳefuhton 7 hæfdon siჳe, 7 hie bedrifon ut on
ane ea 7 moniჳe adrencton. *Her pæs Pleჳemund*
ჳecoren of Jode 7 of eallen his halechen.   10

Anno dcccxci. Her for se here east 7 Earnulf cyninჳ

888⁵. *Æþelred, Æ* is a large capital partly in the margin ;
l added above the line. 889. MS *dccclxxxuiiii*, the last two
minims being above the line. The second line of this annal is
added above in a blank space at the end of the annal 888.

890¹. *abbud*, MS *abb'*. 890⁹. *Her . . . halechen* added by a
later scribe ; *ჳecoren*, MS *ჳecoron*.

---

⁴ *æt Pafian :* Pavia was on the road to Rome and English pilgrims
would pass through it (cf Stevenson 209).

890². *Jodrum :* see annals 878, 886, above.

⁶ *Sant Laudan :* the Danes moved to St-Lô (22 m SW Bayeux)
in autumn 889 (*Annales Vedastini* 67–8) ; they were defeated by
the Bretons in 890 ; thereafter, about All Saints' Day (1 November
890), they went into winter-quarters at Noyen (Somme).

⁹ *on ane ea :* the river is not known, but the Vire has been suggested
(Plummer II. 102), as well as the Couësnon (cf Hoffmann-Hirtz 87n).

⁹ *Her pæs Pleჳemund . . . :* a Canterbury addition (cf Introd.
p. 4). Pleჳemund was a famous Mercian scholar whom Ælfred
had appointed as one of his teachers (*Cura Pastoralis*, ed. H. Sweet,
(EETS 45), 7, and Asser). The interpolation refers to Pleჳemund's
elevation to the Archbishopric of Canterbury.

891. In 891 the Norsemen moved east from Noyen to the Meuse
and in the autumn sought winter-quarters at Louvain on the
R. Dyle ; they were there defeated by Arnulf, but after being

ȝefeaht piðð ðæm rede here ær þa scipu cuomon
mid East-Francum 7 Seaxum 7 Bæȝerum 7 hine
ȝefliemde. 7 þrie Scottas comon to Ælfrede
cyninȝe on anum bate butan elcum ȝereþrum of
Hibernia, þonon hi hi bestelon forþon þe hi poldon
for Ȝodes lufan on elþiodiȝnesse beon, hi ne rohton
hpær. Se bat pæs ȝeporht of þriddan healfre hyde
þe hi on foron, 7 hi namon mid him þæt hi hæfdun
to seofon nihtum mete. 7 þa comon hie ymb uii
niht to londe on Cornpalum 7 foron þa sona to Ælfrede cyninȝe. Þus hie pæron ȝenemnde : Dub-
slane 7 Maccbethu 7 Maelinmun. 7 Swifneh se
betsta lareop þe on Scottum pæs ȝefor.

891[14]. *pæs ȝefor*: followed by the annal number *an dcccxcii* in
the margin of the next line, left blank ; fol. 16b begins 7 *þy ilcan
ȝeare* (see note below). After this there is little margin and the
annal numbers are indented in the text or centred until 897.

dispersed they reassembled at Louvain before the end of the year,
staying there until the autumn of 892 (*Annales Vedastini, ed. cit.*
70, *Annales Fuldenses Contin. ed. cit.* 119, Plummer II. 103). As
Arnulf's victory over the Danes was in November 891, it suggests
that in this annal the chronicler's year began at Christmas ; this
now appears to become the regular mode (cf below). MSS C and D
place this battle in 892 according to the older system of reckoning
the year from 24 September.

2 *pið ðæm rede here :* Plummer II. cvii compares Orosius (*ed. cit.*
124) : *on þæm rædehere.* Cf Introd. p. 7.

4 *þrie Scottas :* 'three Irishmen', i.e. Scots from Ireland. On the
Irish zeal for pilgrimages, often undertaken under very difficult self-
imposed conditions, and the relationship between Ireland and England
cf. Plummer II. 103–5, Hoffmann-Hirtz 88n, and C. H. Slover, *Early
Literary Channels between England and Ireland* (University of Texas
Studies in English, no. 6), 1–56. The three pilgrims have not been
identified, but the names are Irish, *Dubhslaine, Macbeathadh,
Maelinmhain.*

7 *lufan :* from *lufu*, which was sometimes declined as a weak noun
in early West Saxon (cf P. Cosijn, *Altwestsächsische grammatik,*
Haag 1883–8, pt. ii, p. 18).

13 *Spifneh :* Plummer II. 105 identifies him with ' Suibhne mac
Maelumha, an anchorite and scribe of Clonmacnoise ', who died
according to the annals of Ulster (s.a. 890) in 891. The news of
his death was probably brought by the three pilgrims.

14 *on Scottum pæs ȝefor :* the first scribe finished here four

7 þy ilcan ȝeare ofer Eastron, ymbe ȝanȝdaȝas oþþe [15]
ær, æteopde se steorra þe mon on boclæden hæt cometa ;
same men cpeþaþ on Enȝlisc þæt hit sie feaxede steorra,
forþæm þær stent lanȝ leoma of, hpilum on ane healfe,
hpilum on ælce healfe.

Anno dcccxcii.   Her on þysum ȝeare for se micla here, þe
þe ȝefyrn ymbe spræcon, eft of þæm eastrice pestpeard
to Bunnan, 7 þær purdon ȝescipode, spa þæt hie asettan
hie on anne siþ ofer mid horsum mid ealle, 7 þa comon
up on Limene muþan mid ccl scipa ; se muþa is on   5

892. MS *An dcccxciii*, the last *i* being wrongly added by a later
scribe ; the erratic addition of *i* to the year numbers continues to
928, MS 929 (see note below).

892²–892⁴. In the margin a seventeenth-century hand has added
R. Talbotus in suo itinerario transeit hec verba in Latinum, an allusion to *Annotationes in eam partem Antonini itinerarii quae ad
Britanniam pertinent* by Robert Talbot, the sixteenth-century
antiquarian.   892⁴. *hie* MS *him*.   892⁵. *ccl*, MS *ccl hunde*.

---

lines from the bottom of fol. 16a ; in the margin of the next line he
wrote *an dcccxcii* but did not continue.   The rest of the annal is
added by the second scribe on fol. 16b, but he omitted to delete the
year number 892 written by the first scribe.   A later scribe was
misled by this into thinking that the passage about the comet was
892 and proceeded to add 1 to the year properly given as 892, making
it 893 ; this was done with each annal to 929.

[15] *ymbe ȝanȝdaȝas :* Rogation Days, in this year 29–31 May.

[17] *same men . . . :* the other MSS read *sume men* ' some people ' ;
same in this MS has probably arisen from the confusion of *u* and
open *a* in an earlier copy and *sume* should perhaps be restored,
especially as *same* appears to be used only when followed by *swa*.

892. From here until 929, each annalistic year has been wrongly
increased by 1 (cf 891¹⁴n) ; the correct years are restored here
without further note.   See above, p. 10.

[1] *se micla here :* the Danish army, which had been defeated by
Arnulf at Louvain in 891.   They remained in the neighbourhood
of Louvain over the winter (cf 891n) and in the autumn of 892,
according to *Annales Vedastini (ed. cit. 72)*, *Nortmanni vero a
Luvanio regressi, videntes omne regnum fame atteri, relicta Francia
tempore autumni mare transierunt*.   It was famine, not the Louvain
defeat, which drove the Danes back to England.

[3] *asettan . . . on anne siþ :* cf Chronicle 1001 *spa þæt hy up
asetton on ænne siþ ;   hie* restored from other MSS.

[5] *on Limene muþan :* ' the mouth of the Lympne ' ; this is an
old name for the East Rother (Sussex, Kent).   Its course haʳ

eastepeardre Cent æt þæs miclan puda eastende þe
pe Andred hatað ; se pudu is eastlanȝ 7 pestlanȝ hund-
tpelftiȝes mila lanȝ oþþe lenȝra 7 þritiȝes mila brad.
Seo ea þe pe ær ymbe spræcon lið ut of þæm pealda.
On þa ea hi tuȝon up hiora scipu oþ þone peald iiii [1]
mila fram þæm muþan utepeardum 7 þær abræcon an
ȝepeorc inne on þæm fenne ; sæton feapa cirlisce men
on 7 pæs samporht. Þa sona æfter þæm com Hæsten
mid lxxx scipa up on Temese muðan 7 porhte him
ȝepeorc æt Middeltune, 7 se oþer here æt Apuldre.   [1]
Anno dcccxciii.   On þys ȝeare, þæt pæs ymb tpelf monað
þæs þe hie on þæm eastrice ȝepeorc ȝeporht hæfdon,

892[6]. *miclan*, MS *miclam*, originally *miclum*.   3

------

changed considerably, but the old bed of the river was used in the
construction of the Royal Military Canal and passed Appledore ;
it runs into the sea at Rye, but formerly it ran out at Lympne (Kent) ;
cf E. Ekwall, *English River-Names*, Oxford 1928, 243.

[5] MS *ccl hunde scipa*, probably an error for *ccl scipa* ; cf MS E
þridde healf hund scipa.

[7] *Andred :* the great wood was sometimes called *Andredeswealde*
' the wood in Andred ' (cf *Place-Names of Sussex*, EPN VI, 1–2).

[9] *seo ea . . . lið ut of þæm pealda :* Plummer II. cvii compares
Orosius (*ed. cit.* 20) : *Seo Wisle lið út of Weonodland.*

[9] *of þæm pealda :* this again is an allusion to the Wood of Andred ;
it survives as The Weald.   On OE *weald* ' forest-land ', and especially ' high forest-land ', cf A. Mawer, *Chief Elements*, EPN I. i. 63.

[12] *fenne* (A, F), *fænne* (E) ; *fæsten(n)e* (B, C, D) is usually restored
and the passage punctuated *þær abræcon an ȝepeorc. Inne on þæm
fæstenne . . . men on.*   But this introduces a redundant preposition *on.*   The fen is between Rye and Appledore.

[13] *Hæsten* (ON *Hásteinn*), the foster-father of Bjǫrn, a son of
Ragnar Lothbrok ; cf A. Mawer, *The Vikings* (1913), 44–7.

[15] *se oþer here :* the army at the mouth of the Lympne.

893. This annal records one of the most active and skilful campaigns of the Danes.   The essential point in their tactics was the
existence of two separate armies, one at Appledore in the south of
Kent, the other at Milton Royal in the north of Kent.   Ælfred was
thus forced to take up a position between them, but he simplified
matters by making a truce with the Milton army, which then
moved across the Thames to Benfleet in Essex.   The larger force at
Appledore which would then have had to meet Ælfred without
support then left Appledore and attempted to join Hæsten by way
of Berkshire and the Upper Thames valley (see notes below).

Norþhymbre 7 East-Enȝle hæfdon Ælfrede cyninȝe
aþas ȝeseald 7 East-Enȝle foreȝisla ui 7 þeh, ofer þa
treopa, spa oft spa þa oþre herȝas mid ealle heriȝe ut foron, 5
þonne foron hie oþþe mid oþþe on heora healfe. Ond þa
ȝeȝaderade Ælfred cyninȝ his fierd 7 fór þæt he ȝepicode
betpuh þæm tpam herȝum þær þær he niehst rymet
hæfde for pudufæstenne ond for pæterfæstenne, spa
þæt he mehte æȝþerne ȝeræcan ȝif hie æniȝne feld secan 10
polden. þa foron hie siþþan æfter þæm pealda hloþum
7 flocradum bi spa hpaþerre efes spa hit þonne fierdleas
pæs, 7 him mon eac mid oþrum floccum sohte mæstra
daȝa ælce, oþþe on dæȝ oþþe on niht, ȝe of þære fierde
ȝe eac of þæm burȝum. Hæfde se cyninȝ his fierd on tu 15

893⁶. *Ond þa*, MS *on. þa* ; *on* may be read as *an*.
893¹⁴. *oþþe on dæȝ* not in MS.

---

² *on þæm eastrice ȝepeorc :* the *ȝepeorc* was probably the winter
namp of the Danes at Louvain after their defeat by Arnulf (see 891
cotes). *ymb tpelf monað* (l. 1) would mean just over twelve months
from this encampment at Louvain about December 891 to the end
of December 892 or January 893 ; this again suggests that the
chronicler is now changing his years at Christmas.

³ *Norþhymbre 7 East Enȝle :* i.e. the Danes settled in Northumbria (cf 876) and East Anglia (cf 880).

⁵ *þa oþre herȝas :* the armies at Appledore and Milton.

⁶ *þonne foron hie . . . :* ' then they (the Northumbrian and East
Anglian Danes) went out either with the two armies or on their
own account '.

⁶ *Ond þa :* so C, D. MSS A¹, A², B, read *healfe on. þa*.

⁸ *þær he niehst rymet . . . pæterfæstenne :* ' where he could find
a space as convenient as possible for the forest stronghold (at
Appledore) and for the river stronghold (at Milton) '.

¹⁰ *ȝif hie æniȝne feld secan polden :* ' in case they wished to make
for any open-country '. OE *feld* meant ' a great stretch of open,
unenclosed land ' (cf A. Mawer, *Chief Elements*, EPN I. i, 26).

¹¹ *hloþum :* cf 837n.

¹² *efes* MS : for the uninflected form in the locative or dative cf
ham (l. 16 below), and on the locative case cf E. Ekwall, *Namn
och Bygd* xvi. 59 ff. For the sense cf Woodhouse Eaves on the edge
of Charnwood Forest (Leic.).

¹⁵ *burȝum :* Professor Bruce Dickins notes the interesting parallel
from Vegetius, *De Re Militari*, IV. 10 : *castellum parvulum quem
burgum vocant.*

¹⁵ *on tu tonumen :* the plan of dividing the army into two sections.

tonumen, spa þæt hie pæron simle healfe æt ham, healfe
ute, butan þæm monnum þe þa burȝa healdan scoldon.
Ne cóm se here oftor eall ute of þæm setum þonne tuppa,
oþre siþe þa hie ærest to londe comon ær sio fierd ȝesamn-
od pære, oþre siþe þa hie of þæm setum faran poldon. 20
Þa hie ȝefenȝon micle herehyð 7 þa poldon ferian norþ-
peardes ofer Temese in on East-Seaxe onȝean þa scipu,
þa forrad sio fierd hie foran 7 him pið ȝefeaht æt Fearn-
hamme 7 þone here ȝefliemde 7 þa herehyþa ahreddon,
7 hie fluȝon ofer Temese buton ælcum forda, þa up be 25
Colne on anne iȝȝað. Þa besæt sio fierd hie þær utan
þa hpile þe hie þær lenȝest mete hæfdon. Ac hi hæfdon
þa heora stemn ȝesetenne 7 hiora mete ȝenotudne
7 pæs se cynȝ þa þiderpeardes on fære mid þære
scire þe mid him fierdedon. Þa he þa pæs þider- 30
peardes 7 sio oþeru fierd pæs hampeardes 7 ða Deniscan
sæton þær behindan, forþæm hiora cyninȝ pæs ȝepundod
on þæm ȝefeohte, þæt hi hine ne mehton ferian, þa
ȝeȝaderedon þa þe in Norþhymbrum buȝeað 7 on East-
Enȝlum sum hund scipa 7 foron suð ymbutan 7 sum 35

893[24]. *ahreddon, a* smudged. 893[28]. *Ac*, so MS. *þa heora stemn*
begins fol. 17a.

---

to be on active service alternately, was intended to preserve the
continuity of labour in agriculture and other domestic pursuits;
the weakness of the system was in the change from one division to
the other (cf ll. 26–9 below, from which it is clear that the Danes
were only prevented from taking the opportunity by the injuries
of their king). The plan may have been suggested to Ælfred by a
passage in Orosius (*ed. cit.* 46) : *hie* [the Amazons] *heora here on tu
todældon, oþer æt ham beon heora lond to healdanne, oðer ut faran to
winnanne* ; cf F. G. M. Beck, EHR xxi. 766, H. M. Chadwick,
Origin of the English Nation (Cambridge 1924), 158 ff.

[22] *onȝean scipu :* to meet the ships by which Hæsten and the
Milton army were crossing to Benfleet (cf l. 38).

[26] *on anne iȝȝað :* Thorney Island (Hertfordshire) ; cf F. M.
Stenton, EHR xxvii. 512.

[27] *hæfdon . . . heora stemn ȝesetenne :* note the agreement in case
and number between the p.pt. and the object of *hæfdon ; ȝesetenne*
is not the complement of *hæfdon ;* so too with *mete ȝenotudne :*
' they had (or ' they were there with ') their tour of duty complete
and their food consumed '.

feopertiȝ scipa norþ ymbutan 7 ymbsæton an ȝepeorc
on Defnascire be þære norþsæ ; 7 þa þe suð ymbutan foron
ymbsæton Exancester. Þa se cynȝ þæt hierde, þa þende
he hine þest þið Exanceastres mid ealre þære fierde, buton
spiþe ȝepaldenum dæle eastepeardes þæs folces. Þa **40**
foron forð oþþe hie comon to Lundenbyrȝ 7 þa mid þæm
burȝparum 7 þæm fultume þe him þestan cóm foron east
to Beamfleote. Þæs Hæsten þa þær cumen mid his
herȝe, þe ær æt Middeltune sæt, 7 eac se micla here þæs
þa þær tocumen, þe ær on Limene muþan sæt æt Apuldre. **45**
Hæfde Hæsten ær ȝeporht þæt ȝepeorc æt Beamfleote 7 þæs
þa ut afaren on herȝaþ 7 þæs se micla here æt ham. Þa
foron hie to 7 ȝefliemdon þone here 7 þæt ȝepeorc abræcon
7 ȝenamon eal þæt þær binnan þæs, ȝe on feo, ȝe on pifum,
ȝe eac on bearnum, 7 brohton eall in to Lundenbyrȝ 7 þa **50**
scipu eall oðþe tobræcon oþþe forbærndon oþþe to Lun-
denbyriȝ brohton oþþe to Hrofesceastre. 7 Hæstenes
pif 7 his suna tpeȝen mon brohte to þæm cyninȝe 7 he
hi him eft aȝeaf, forþæm þe hiora þæs oþer his ȝodsunu,
oþer Æðeredes ealdormonnes. Hæfdon hi hiora onfanȝen **55**
ær Hæsten to Beamfleote come 7 he him hæfde ȝeseald

---

[37] *be þære norþsæ :* the Bristol Channel.

[40] *ȝepaldenum dæle . . . :* ' a small number of people remaining
in the east '. On the meaning of *ȝepalden,* ' small, insignificant ',
cf BT, Plummer II. 109. Florence of Worcester (ed. B. Thorpe,
London 1848) I. iii, has : *paucis tamen ad debellandum quem
insequebatur hostem relictis.*

[46] *ær :* i.e. before the arrival of the Appledore army, which had
now been defeated at Farnham and besieged in the Colne. Hæsten's
move to Benfleet probably induced the Danes to dash from Appledore at once.

[48] *hie :* i.e. the *ȝepalden dæl* of l. 40.

[56] *ær Hæsten . . . to Beamfleote come :* the chronicler is recording
in order the movements of the Appledore army, at the same time
fitting in incidents in Hæsten's campaign, which is somewhat
obscured by this method of narration. Whilst at Milton Hæsten
had made a truce with Ælfred, giving hostages (ll. 56–7) in return
for money (l. 57) and Hæsten's sons were baptized (ll. 54–5). Ælfred
was then free to deal with the Appledore army, which immediately
left the district. Hæsten seizing his opportunity broke the truce
and crossed to Benfleet (l. 43), made an encampment (ll. 46, 59).

ʒislas 7 aðas 7 se cynʒ him eac þel feoh sealde 7 eac spa
þa he þone cniht aʒef 7 þæt þif. Ac sona spa hie to
Beamfleote comon 7 þæt ʒepeorc ʒeporct pæs, spa herʒode
he on his rice þone ilcan ende þe Æþered his cumpæder ⁶⁶
healdan sceolde, 7 eft oþre siþe he pæs on herʒað ʒelend
on þæt ilce rice þa þa mon his ʒepeorc abræc. þa se
cyninʒ hine þa þest þende mid þære fierde pið Exancestres,
spa ic ær sæde, 7 se here þa burʒ beseten hæfde, þa he
þær to ʒefaren pæs, þa eodon hie to hiora scipum. þa he ⁶
þa pið þone here þær pæst abisʒod pæs 7 þa herʒas pæron
þa ʒeʒaderode beʒen to Sceobyriʒ on East-Seaxum 7 þær
ʒepeorc þorhtun, foron beʒen ætʒædere up be Temese 7
him com micel eaca to, æʒþer ʒe of East-Enʒlum, ʒe of
Norþhymbrum. Foron þa up be Temese oþþæt hie ⁷
ʒedydon æt Sæferne, þa up be Sæferne. þa ʒeʒaderode
Æþered ealdormon 7 Æþelm ealdorman 7 Æþelnoþ ealdorman 7 þa cinʒes þeʒnas þe þa æt ham æt þæm ʒepeorcum
pæron, of ælcre byriʒ be eastan Pedredan, ʒe be þestan
Sealpuda ʒe be eastan, ʒe eac be norþan Temese 7 be ⁷
þestan Sæfern, ʒe eac sum dæl þæs Norð-Þeal cynnes. þa

893⁵⁹. *Beamfleote*, MS *bleam fleote* ; *-þorct*, *t* added above line ;
this begins fol. 17b. 893⁶⁰. *on* added above line by a later scribe.

---

and went harrying (l. 59). The Appledore Danes finally arrived at
Benfleet (l. 44) and Hæsten went pillaging again (ll. 47, 61). In
Hæsten's absence, the English captured the camp at Benfleet (ll. 48,
62) and took Hæsten's wife and two sons (l. 53) ; these were restored
to Hæsten (l. 54), along with a fresh payment of money (l. 57-8).

⁵⁸ *Ac sona spa . . . :* 'As soon as they (Hæsten and his army)
came to Benfleet and the encampment was made, he (Hæsten)
harried in that district of his (Ælfred's) kingdom that his gossip
Æþered was to protect.' Professor Bruce Dickins notes from the
Laws of William the Conqueror 2 the equation of *ende* with *ballia*.

⁶⁴ *ær :* i.e. in ll. 38-9.

⁶⁶ *þa herʒas :* these were (1) the Danes defeated at Benfleet in
Hæsten's absence (the Appledore Danes) and (2) Hæsten's army,
which had, according to the Annals of St Neots (Stevenson 141),
repaired the encampment at Benfleet after the English had left
for London (l. 50). They had foregathered at Shoebury.

⁷⁶ *þæs Norð-Þeal cynnes :* on the alliance of Welsh and English
at this period cf B G. Charles, *Old Norse Relations with Wales*,
1934, 15-16.

hie þa ealle ȝeȝaderode pæron, þa offoron hie þone here
hindan æt Buttinȝtune on Sæferne staþe, 7 hine þær
utan besæton on ælce healfe on anum fæstenne. Þa
hie ða fela pucena sæton on tpa healfe þære é 7 se cynȝ 80
pæs pest on Defnum piþ þone sciphere, þa pæron hie mid
metelieste ȝepæȝde 7 hæfdon micelne dæl þara horsa freten
7 þa oþre pæron hunȝre acpolen, þa eodon hie ut to ðæm
monnum þe on easthealfe þære é picodon 7 him piþ ȝefuhton, 7 þa Cristnan hæfdon siȝe ; 7 þær pearð Ordheh 85
cyninȝes þeȝn ofslæȝen 7 eac moniȝe oþre cyninȝes þeȝnas
ofslæȝen, 7 se dæl þe þær apeȝ com purdon on fleame
ȝenerede. Þa hie on East Seaxe comon to hiora ȝepeorce
7 to hiora scipum, þa ȝeȝaderade sio laf eft of East-Enȝlum
7 of Norðhymbrum micelne here onforan pinter 7 befæston 90
hira pif 7 hira scipu 7 hira feoh on East-Enȝlum 7 foron
ánstreces dæȝes 7 nihtes þæt hie ȝedydon on anre pestre

893⁸⁰. *þære é*, MS *þæré*. 893⁸¹. *pæs pest*, MS *pæst*, with *pes*
added above *t*. 893⁸⁶. *þeȝnas*, *as* added by later scribe.
893⁹⁰. *norðhymbrū* begins fol. 18a.

---

⁷⁸ *æt Buttingtune :* identified with Buttington Tump near Chepstow,
which is preferable to Buttington near Welshpool, as the phrase *on
tpa healfe þære é* (l. 80) could hardly refer to the Severn Estuary, but
it might well refer to the Wye where it joins the Severn at Buttington
Tump ; cf Plummer II. 109, and B. G. Charles, *op. cit.* 16.

⁸³ *þa oþre :* the remaining horses.

⁸⁶ *þeȝnas ofslæȝen :* after these words other MSS add 7 *þara
Deniscra þær pearð spiþe mycel ȝesleȝen* (MS B). Plummer I. 87n and
A. J. Wyatt, *An Anglo-Saxon Reader* (Cambridge 1919) 205 suggests
that this should be restored in A.

⁹² *ánstreces :* the meaning is not certain. In the Cura Pastoralis
anstræc means ' resolute, determined ', which used adverbially
would be satisfactory here. It is usual, however, to give it a
developed temporal sense in this context, ' at one stretch, continu-
ously ' (possibly suggested by modern English *stretch* recorded in
this sense from 1541, NED). But ME *strek, strik*, as in the *Pricke
of Conscience*, l. 2623 (*þe synful saul þan gas strik to helle*) suggest
rather ' straight, direct '. They probably went by Watling Street.

⁹² *anre pestre ceastre :* the deserted city is *Leȝaceaster*, Chester
on the Dee, which was called by Bede *ciuitatem Legionum, quae a
gente Anglorum Leȝacaestir, a Brettonibus autem rectius Carlegion
appellatur* ; it was in Roman times the station of the Twentieth

ceastre on Þirhealum, seo is Leʒaceaster ʒehaten. Þa
ne mehte seo fird hie ná hindan offaran, ær hie pæron inne
on þæm ʒepeorce ; besæton þeah þæt ʒepeorc utan sume ⁹
tpeʒen daʒas 7 ʒenamon ceapes eall þæt þær buton pæs 7 þa
men ofsloʒon þe hie foran forridan mehton butan ʒepeorce
7 þæt corn eall forbærndon 7 mid hira horsum fretton on
ælcre efenehðe. 7 þæt pæs ymb tpelf monað þæs þe hie
ær hider ofer sæ comon. ¹⁰

Anno dcccxciv.

ONd þa sona æfter þæm on ðys ʒere fór se here of Þírheale
in on Norð-Þealas, forþæm hie ðær sittan ne mehton ;
þæt pæs forðy þe hie pæron benumene æʒðer ʒe þæs
ceapes, ʒe þæs cornes, ðe hie ʒeherʒod hæfdon. Þa hie ða
eft ut of Norð-Þealum pendon mid þære herehyðe þe
hie ðær ʒenumen hæfdon, þa foron hie ofer Norðhymbra
lond 7 East-Enʒla, spa spa seo fird hie ʒeræcan ne mehte,
oþþæt hie comon on East-Seaxna lond eastepeard on an
iʒland þæt is ute on þære sæ, þæt is Meresiʒ haten. 7 þa
se here eft hampeard pende, þe Exanceaster beseten
hæfde, þa herʒodon hie up on Suð-Seaxum neah Cisseceastre,
7 þa burʒpare hie ʒefliemdon 7 hira moniʒ hund ofsloʒon
7 hira scipu sumu ʒenamon.

Ða þy ilcan ʒere onforan pinter þa Deniscan þe on Meres-
iʒe sæton tuʒon hira scipu up on Temese 7 þa up on
Lyʒan. Þæt pæs ymb tpa ʒer þæs þe hie hider ofer sæ
comon.

894. MS *Añ dcccxcv*, *v* over an erasure ; *ONd*, a large *O* enclos-
ing *N*. 894¹⁴. *Ða*, MS *ða*, perhaps by a later hand ; *ð* is a large
letter. 894¹⁵. *up* (1st), MS *úp*. 895. MS *Añ dcccxcvi*, *i* being added
by a later scribe ; this begins fol. 18b.

Legion (Plummer II. 110). According to Plummer (*Bede's Histor.
Eccles.* II. 77), its desolation goes back to the Battle of Chester
in 616.
⁹⁹ *efenehðe*, other MSS *efennehþe*, ' neighbourhood ', a derivative
(like *hiehþ(u)*, Anglian *hehþ(u)* ' height ' from *heah*) from the preposition *efen-neah* ' equally near ' (BT) ; cf OIcel *jafn-nǽr*.
894⁹. *an iʒland . . . Meresiʒ :* Mersea Island ; cf *Place-Names
of Essex* (EPN XI), 320.

Anno dcccxcv.

On þy ilcan ʒere porhte se foresprecena here ʒepeorc be
Lyʒean xx mila bufan Lundenbyriʒ. Þa þæs on sumera
foron micel dæl þara burʒpara 7 eac spa oþres folces
þæt hie ʒedydon æt þara Deniscana ʒepeorce, 7 þær
purdon ʒefliemde 7 sume feoper cyninʒes þeʒnas ofslæʒene.   5
Þa þæs on hærfeste þa picode se cynʒ on neapeste þære
byriʒ, þa hpile þe hie hira corn ʒerypon, þæt þa Deniscan
him ne mehton þæs ripes forpiernan. Þa sume dæʒe rad
se cynʒ up bi þære éæ 7 ʒehapade hpær mon mehte þa
éa forpyrcan, þæt hie ne mehton þa scipu ut brenʒan.   10
7 hie ða spa dydon ; porhton ða tú ʒepeorc on tpa healfe
þære éas. Þa hie ða þæt ʒepeorc furþum onʒunnen hæfdon
7 þærto ʒepicod hæfdon, þa onʒet se here þæt hie ne
mehton þa scipu ut brenʒan. Þa forleton hie hie 7 eodon
ofer land þæt hie ʒedydon æt Cpatbrycʒe be Sæfern 7   15
þær ʒeperc porhton. Þa rad seo fird pest æfter þæm
heriʒe 7 þa men of Lundenbyriʒ ʒefetedon þa scipu, 7 þa
ealle þe hie álædan ne mehton tobræcon, 7 þa þe þær stæl-
pyrðe pæron binnan Lundenbyriʒ ʒebrohton. 7 þa Deniscan hæfdon hira pif befæst innan East-Enʒle ær hie ut of   20
þæm ʒepeorce foron. Þa sæton hie þone pinter æt
Cpatbrycʒe. Þæt þæs ymb þreo ʒer þæs þe hie on Limene
muðan comon hider ofer sǽ.

Anno dcccxcvi.

Ða þæs on sumera on ðysum ʒere tofór se here, sum on
East-Enʒle, sum on Norðhymbre, 7 þa þe feohlease pæron

896⁴. *þonces* begins fol. 19a.

895¹. *On þy ilcan ʒere :* the use of *ilcan* (in all MSS) is probably
due to the annal 894 having already recorded (l. 10) the autumn
movement of the Danes up the Lea.

⁹ Ælfred's strategy, it is thought (Plummer II. 110), was suggested by Orosius' account of Cyrus and the Euphrates (Orosius,
ed. cit. 74).

¹⁵ *æt Cpatbrycʒe :* Bridgenorth (Shropshire) ; Quat and Quatford
are a little to the south (Plummer II. 110).

896¹. Apart from one or two raids, the departure of the Danes to
East Anglia, Northumbria and the Seine marks the end of Ælfred's
Danish wars.

him þær scipu beʒeton 7 suð ofer sǽ foron to Siʒene. Næfde
se here, Ʒodes þonces, Anʒelcyn ealles forspiðe ʒebrocod.
Ac hie pæron micle spiþor ʒebrocede on þæm þrim ʒearum ⁵
mid ceapes cpilde 7 monna, ealles spiþost mid þæm þæt
maniʒe þara selestena cynʒes þena þe þær on londe
pæron forðferdon on þæm þrim ʒearum ; þara pæs sum
Spiðulf biscop on Hrofesceastre, 7 Ceolmund ealdormon
on Cent 7 Beorhtulf ealdormon on East-Seaxum 7 Þulfred ¹⁰
ealdormon on Hamtunscire 7 Ealhheard biscop æt Dorceceastre 7 Eadulf cynʒes þeʒn on Suð-Seaxum 7 Beorn-
ulf picʒerefa on Þinteceastre 7 Ecʒulf cynʒes horsþeʒn
7 maniʒe eac him þeh ic ða ʒeðunʒnestan nemde. Þy
ilcan ʒeare drehton þa herʒas on East-Enʒlum 7 on ¹⁵
Norðhymbrum Þest-Seaxna lond spiðe be þæm suðstæðe
mid stælherʒum, ealra spiþust mid ðæm æscum þe hie
fela ʒeara ær timbredon. Þa het Ælfred cynʒ timbran
lanʒscipu onʒen ða æscas ; þa pæron fulneah tu spa lanʒe
spa þa oðru ; sume hæfdon lx ara, sume má ; þa pæron ²⁰
æʒðer ʒe spiftran ʒe unpealtran ʒe eac hieran þonne þa
oðru. Næron napðer ne on Fresisc ʒescæpene ne on
Denisc, bute spa him selfum ðuhte þæt hie nytpyrðoste beon
meahten. Þa æt sumum cirre þæs ilcan ʒeares comon
þær sex scipu to Þiht 7 þær micel yfel ʒedydon, æʒðer ʒe ²⁵
on Defenum ʒe pelhpær be ðæm sǽriman. Þa het se
cynʒ faran mid niʒonum tó þara nipena scipa 7 forforon
him þone muðan foran on utermere. Þa foron hie mid
þrim scipum ut onʒen hie 7 þreo stodon æt ufepeardum

896¹³. picʒerefa, MS picʒefera. 896³¹. þa ʒefenʒon begins fol. 19b.

---

³ *to Siʒene :* the return of the Danes to the Seine in five large
vessels (*barchis*) is recorded in the *Annales Vedastini (ed. cit.* 78).

¹¹ *æt Dorceceastre :* the usual preposition is *on* ; Plummer II. III
suggests that *æt* is used here because Ealhheard was Bishop of
Leicester and his see was moved to Dorchester (Oxford), because
of the Danes.

¹⁷ *æscum ;* æsc in the sense ' boat ' is probably a loan from
ON *askr* (cf Cleasby-Vigfusson, *Icelandic Dictionary,* s.v.).

²⁸ A. J. Wyatt, *An Anglo-Saxon Reader,* 206, suggests Poole Harbour as a possible site for this skirmish. The six Danish vessels
entered the harbour and then nine English vessels blockaded the
entrance from the open sea (*on uter-mere*). Three of the Danish

þæm muðan on dryȝum ; pæron þa men uppe on londe of [30]
ágáne. Þa ȝefenȝon hie þara þreora scipa tú æt ðæm
muðan utepeardum 7 þa men ofsloȝon 7 þæt án oðpand ;
on þæm pæron eac þa men ofslæȝene buton fifum ; þa
comon forðy onpeȝ ðe ðara oþerra scipu ásæton. Þa purdon eac spiðe uneðelice áseten ; þreo ásæton on ða healfe [35]
þæs deopes ðe ða Deniscan scipu aseten pæron 7 þa oðru
eall on oþre healfe, þæt hira ne mehte nan to oðrum. Ac
ða þæt pæter pæs áhebbad fela furlanȝa from þæm scipum,
þa eodon ða Deniscan from þæm þrim scipum to þæm
oðrum þrim þe on hira healfe beebbade pæron, 7 hie þa [40]
þær ȝefuhton. Þær pearð ofslæȝen Lucumon cynȝes
ȝerefa 7 Þulfheard Friesa 7 Æbbe Friesa 7 Æðelhere
Friesa 7 Æðelferð cynȝes ȝeneat, 7 ealra monna Fresiscra
7 Enȝliscra lxii 7 þara Deniscena cxx. Þa cóm þæm
Deniscum scipum þeh ær flod to, ær þa Cristnan mehten [45]
hira ut áscufan, 7 hie forðy ut oðreopon. Þa pæron hie to
þæm ȝesarȝode, þæt hie ne mehton Suð-Seaxna lond utan

896³⁴. onpeȝ, MS onpéȝ.   896⁴⁶. áscufan, f altered from t.

ships had grounded at the upper end of the harbour (on the north side) and the other three went out to meet the English. Two of them were seized and the third escaped with five men because the English had run aground. Cf. G. P. Krapp, MLN xix. 232–4.

[33] *þa comon forðy . . .* : ' these (five) escaped because the ships of the others (the English) had run aground '.

[34] *þa purdon . . .* : ' These (i.e. the English ships) had run aground awkwardly.'

[42] *ȝerefa* : bailiff, sheriff ; a *cynȝes ȝerefa*, was a person of higher rank. On these terms cf W. A. Morris, EHR xxxi. 20–40 ; but the MS *ȝefera* ' companion ' may be correct here ; cf *cynȝes ȝeneat* (l. 43).

[42] *Þulfheard Friesa . . .* : these were Frisian sailors employed by Ælfred to man his new warships (cf Plummer II. 111–12, and on the names of these Frisians cf T. Forssner, *Continental-Germanic Personal Names in English*, Uppsala 1916, xlv–xlvii, &c). The Frisians were famous sailors ; cf *Gnomic Verses* 95 ff : *Leof pilcuma Frysan pife þonne flota stondeð*, &c.

[43] *cynȝes ȝeneat* : originally *ȝeneat* ' companion ' seems to have been a tenant of low rank, but a *cynȝes ȝeneat* had the same wergild as a *cyninȝes þeȝn* ; cf H. M. Chadwick, *Anglo-Saxon Institutions* 138–9.

beropan, ac hira þær tu sæ on lond þearp, 7 þa men mon
lædde to Pinteceastre to þæm cynʒe 7 he hie ðær ahon het.
7 þa men comon on East-Enʒle þe on þæm ánum scipe [50]
pæron, spiðe forpundode. Þy ilcan sumera forpearð nolæs
þonne xx scipa mid monnum mid ealle be þæm suðriman.
Þy ilcan ʒere forðferde Pulfric cynʒes horsðeʒn, se pæs
eac Pealhʒerefa.

Anno dcccxcvii.　Her on þysum ʒere ʒefor Æðelm Piltunscire ealdormon niʒon nihtum ær middum sumere,
7 her forðferde Heahstan se pæs on Lundenne
biscop.

Anno dcccc.　Her ʒefor Ælfred Aþulfinʒ syx nihtum ær
ealra haliʒra mæssan. Se pæs cyninʒ ofer eall
Onʒelcyn butan ðæm dæle þe under Dena onpalde
pæs, 7 he heold þæt rice oþrum healfum læs þe
xxx pintra. 7 þa fenʒ Eadpeard his sunu to rice. [5]

896[54]. *Pealhʒerefa*, MS *pealh ʒe fera.*

897. In the margin opposite this annal are the year numbers
898, 899, 900 (altered by a later scribe from 897, 898, 899, respectively, as above).　897[3]. *forðferde* begins fol. 20a.

900. In the margin opposite the first two lines of this annal are
the year numbers 901, 902, both altered from 900, 901 (i.e. *dcccc,
dccgci*), respectively.

900[1]. *Ælfred ;* a small cross above the name.

900[5]. *Eadpeard*, a large cross in the margin opposite the name.

---

[54] *Pealhʒerefa*, ' the Welsh sheriff ', usually taken to mean the
sheriff in charge of the Welsh Marches, the leader of the *Wealh-
færeld*. But cf L. M. Larson, *The King's Household in England
before the Norman Conquest* (Bulletin of Univ. of Wisconsin, no. 100,
1924), 178.

900. The year of Ælfred's death is variously stated to be 899 and
900 (W. H. Stevenson, EHR xii. 71 ff, Plummer II. 71 ff). His
accession was in April 871 (Æþered's death was ' after Easter ',
cf 871[30]), and his reign lasted ' one and a half less than thirty years ' ;
this would make the date of his death 26 October 899. If the old
system of reckoning the year from September 24 was in use here,
this date would normally fall within the annalistic year 900 ; cf
M. L. R. Beaven, EHR xxxii. 517, and R. W. Chambers, *England
before the Norman Conquest* (1926), xxiii–xxiv.

BIBLIOGRAPHY

(This list is concerned chiefly with the Parker MS, but some reference is made to works dealing with other MSS, and for the student's convenience a few general works on the history of the period are included where considerable use is made of the Chronicles. The list does not aim at completeness.)

I. BIBLIOGRAPHICAL LISTS

1862 T. D. Hardy, *A Descriptive Catalogue of materials relating to the History of Great Britain and Ireland* (Rolls Series), I. 651 ff.

1885 *R. Wülcker, *Grundriss zur Geschichte der angelsächsischen Litteratur*, 440–50

1892–9 *C. Plummer, *Two of the Saxon Chronicles Parallel*, II. xi–xvi, cxvii–cxxxvii

1896 *K. Horst, *Zur Kritik der altenglischen Annalen* (Darmstadt), 3 ff.

1908 *A. Brandl, in *Grundriss der Germanischen Philologie* 1061–2

1915 C. Gross, *Sources and Literature of English History from the earliest times to about* 1485, 235–7

1931 L. J. Paetow, *Guide to the Study of Mediæval History* (rev. by F. P. Magoun) (New York), 46–53

1931 A. H. Heusinkveld and E. T. Bashe, *Bibliographical Guide to Old English* (University of Iowa Studies IV. 5), 112–13

1933 *M. Hoffmann-Hirtz, *Une Chronique Anglo-Saxonne* (Strasburg), 133–43 and notes

II. EDITIONS

(All the early editions of the chronicles were composite texts, such as 1643 A. Wheloc, *Chronologia Anglo-Saxonica* (Cambridge), 1692 *A. Gibson, *Chronicon Saxonicum* (Oxford), 1823 *J. Ingram, *The Saxon Chronicle*, 1848 R. Price, *Monumenta Historica Britannica*.

1865 *J. Earle, *Two of the Saxon Chronicles*

1861 *B. Thorpe, *The Anglo-Saxon Chronicle* (Rolls Series)

1892 *C. Plummer, *Two of the Saxon Chronicles Parallel* (the annals 787–1001 being also published separately)

There are extracts in many readers, based largely upon Thorpe and Plummer. The following are amongst the more important:

1919 *A. J. Wyatt, *An Anglo-Saxon Reader*

1922 H. Sweet, *An Anglo-Saxon Reader* (9th ed. rev. by C. T. Onions)

1928 W. J. Sedgefield, *An Anglo-Saxon Book of Prose*

53

1929 W. A. Craigie, *Specimens of Anglo-Saxon Prose, III. British and Anglo-Saxon History* (Edinburgh)

1929 *G. P. Krapp and A. G. Kennedy, *An Anglo-Saxon Reader* (New York)

1930 G. T. Flom, *Introductory Old English Grammar and Reader* (Boston)

1931 M. Förster, *Altenglisches Lesebuch* (4th ed.)

III. STUDIES AND NOTES
Works cited above marked *

1872 L. Theopold, *Kritische Untersuchungen über die Quellen zur angelsächsischen Geschichte des achten Jahrhunderts* (Lemgo)

1886 E. Kube, *Die Wortstellung in der Sachsenchronik* (*Parker-hs.*)

1889 M. Kupferschmidt, ESt xiii. 165–187

1894 D. Abegg, *Zur Entwicklung der historischen Dichtung bei den Angelsachsen* (Quellen und Forschungen 73)

1896–9 K. Horst, ESt xxii. 447–450, xxv. 195

1901 H. M. Blain, *Syntax of the Verb in the Anglo-Saxon Chronicle*

1902 C. Plummer, *The Life and Times of Alfred the Great*

1904 G. P. Krapp, MLN xix. 232–4

1904 W. H. Stevenson, *Asser's Life of King Alfred*

1905 H. M. Chadwick, *Studies on Anglo-Saxon, Institutions*

1906 F. G. M. Beck, EHR xxi. 766

1906 W. A. Robertson, *Tempus und Modus in der ae. Chronik* (Marburg)

1908 W. G. Collingwood, *Scandinavian Britain*

1908 ff. H. H. Howorth, *The Anglo-Saxon Chronicle, its Origin and History*, Archæological Journal lxv. 141–204, lxvi. 105–44, lxix. 312–70, lxxiii. 1–170

1910 J. H. Clapham, EHR xxv. 287

1911 A. G. van Hamel, *De Oudeste Keltiske en Angelsaksiske Geschiedbronnen* (Middelburg)

1911 ff. J. Hoops, *Reallexikon der germanischen Altertumskunde* (especially IV. 63–6)

1912 M. R. James, *A Catalogue of the Manuscripts in Corpus Christi College, Cambridge*, (Cambridge) I. 395 ff.

1912 F. M. Stenton, EHR xxvii. 512

1913 A. F. Major, *Early Wars of Wessex*

1913 A. Mawer, *The Vikings*

1914 W. Roth, *Die Wortstellung in aussage hauptsatz ags. original prosa* (Berlin)

1914 G. C. Donald, *Zur Entwicklung des Prosastils in der Sachsenchronik* (Marburg)

1915 G. Rübens, *Parataxe und Hypotaxe in dem ältesten Teil der Sachsenchronik* (Morsbach Studien 56)

1918 M. L. R. Beaven, EHR xxxiii. 328–42

BIBLIOGRAPHY

1918   G. B. Grundy, *The Saxon Battlefields in Wiltshire*, Archæological Journal lxxv. 188–92
1922   F. Viglione, *Studio critico-filologico su l'Anglo-Saxon Chronicle* (Pavia)
1923   J. A. Robinson, *Times of St. Dunstan*
1924   H. M. Chadwick, *Origin of the English Nation* (2nd impr.)
1924 ff. Publications of the English Place-Name Society
1925   A. Mawer, *Some Place-name identifications in the Anglo-Saxon Chronicles* (Palaestra 147)
1925   F. M. Stenton, in *Essays in Mediæval History presented to T. F. Tout* (Manchester)
1926   E. Classen and F. E. Harmer, *An Anglo-Saxon Chronicle* (Manchester)
1926   R. L. Poole, *Chronicles and Annals*
1927   W. G. Collingwood, ' Christian Vikings ', Antiquity i. 172–80
1928   R. W. Chambers, *England before the Norman Conquest*
1928   E. Ekwall, *English River-Names*
1930   F. P. Magoun (orig. by F. B. Gummere), *Founders of England* (New York)
1930   T. D. Kendrick, *A History of the Vikings*
       G. P. Baker, *The Fighting Kings of Wessex*
1931   O. G. S. Crawford, Antiquity v. 441–58
1933   Marie Hoffmann-Hirtz, *Une Chronique Anglo-Saxonne*
1934   T. D. Kendrick, Saga-Book of the Viking Society, xi. 61–70
1934   B. G. Charles, *Old Norse Relations with Wales* (Cardiff)
1935   R. H. Hodgkin, *A History of the Anglo-Saxons*.
1935   F. P. Magoun, *Territorial, Place- and River-names in the Old English Chronicle* (Harvard Studies and Notes in Philology, xviii. 69 ff.).

IV. TRANSLATIONS

(There are many translations of the Chronicle, but they are mostly composite translations, such as 1643 A. Wheloc, *Chronologia Anglo-Saxonica* (in Latin), 1692 A. Gibson, *Chronicon Saxonicum* (Latin transl.), 1819 A. Gurney, *Saxon Chronicle* (privately circulated), 1823 J. Ingram, *The Anglo-Saxon Chronicle* (reprinted in Everyman's Library 1912), 1847 J. A. Giles, *Bede's Ecclesiastical History and the Anglo-Saxon Chronicle* (Bohn), 1853 J. Stevenson, *The Church Historians of England* (vol. II, pt. 1), 1861 B. Thorpe, *The Anglo-Saxon Chronicle* (vol. II), 1909 E. E. C. Gomme, *The Anglo-Saxon Chronicle*, 1922 F. Viglione, *Studio critico-filologico* (Pavia, as above), *The Saxon Chronicle, from 800–1001* (University Tutorial Press, Cambridge).)

1928   R. W. Chambers, *England before the Norman Conquest* (selections, translated from single MSS)
1933   M. Hoffmann-Hirtz, *Une Chronique Anglo-Saxonne* (in French ; the only complete translation of the Parker MS)

GLOSSARY

In the Glossary words will be found under the forms in which
they occur, except that nouns and adjectives (excluding irregular
comparatives, &c) will be found under the nom.sg. (masc.) and
verbs under the infinitive (except that the present forms of ' to be '
will be found under *beon*, the pret. forms under *wæs*) ; pronouns
under the nom.sg.masc. (except the 1st and 2nd pers. of the personal
pronouns which will be found under the nom.sg. or the nom.pl.
as the case may be). Irregular grammatical or phonological forms
likely to offer difficulty are noted in their proper place with cross-
references to the words under which they are dealt with. References where given are to annals or in the longer annals to annals
and lines. When the reference is followed by * it indicates a restored
or emended form and when followed by n it is a reference to the
appropriate note. The order of letters is alphabetical, but *æ* is
treated as a separate letter after *a* ; *þ, ð* after *t*. The OE characters
ƿ, ʒ, p are replaced by *æ, g, w*. The prefix *ge-* is always ignored in
the arrangement of the glossary. For abbreviations see *Deor*
(ed. Kemp Malone) p. 32 or *Waldere* (ed. F. Norman), p. 49.

A

abbud, *m.a-stem, ABBOT* 890[1*]

ābisgian, *w.v.*(2), occupy, en-
gage, 893[66]

ābrecan, *v.*(5), [ABREAK]; storm,
attack, 860, 892[11]

ac, *conj.* [AC] ; but 893[58]

ācwelan, *v.*(4), [A + QUELE] ;
die, perish, 893[83]

ādrǣfan, *w.v.*(1b), [ADREFE] ;
drive away, banish 874, 878

ādrencan, *w.v.*(1b), [ADRENCH] ;
drown (*trans.*) 890

ādrincan, *v.*(3), [ADRINK] ; to
be drowned 853

āebbian, *w.v.*(2), [A + EBB] ;
ebb away, recede ; **ahebbad**,
ppt. 896[38]

āfaran, *v.*(6), [AFARE] ; go, depart, 894

āflīeman, *w.v.*(1b), [AFLEME] ;
put to flight, expel, 836

āgan,*pret.-pres.*(7), [OWE] ; own.
sige ahton, had the victory 833

āgān, *anom.v.*, [AGO] ; go away
896[31]

āgiefan,*v.*(5), [AGIVE] ; give up,
restore ; **agef**, *p.t.* 893[58]

āhebbad, see **āebbian.**

āhōn, *v.*(7), [AHANG] ; to hang
896[49]

āhreddan, *w.v.*(1a), [AREDDE] ;
rescue 893[24*]

ālǣdan, *w.v.*(1b), take away

ald, *adj.* OLD 885[31]; the Elder
(*byname*) 871[17]

56

aldorman, all, see **ealdormon, eall**

ān, *num.* ONE 878[18], 879[4], 885[16]; *indef.art.* A 874[7], 879[3]*; *adj.* alone 887[11]; *pron.* ONE 875[9], 896[32]

andlanᵹ, see **onlonᵹ**

ānlīpiᵹ, *adj.* [ONLEPY]; single, solitary, 871[40]n

ānstreces, *adv.* direct 893[92]n

ār, *f.ō-stem,* OAR 896[20]

āscūfan, *v.(2),* push off 896[46]

āsettan, *w.v.(1a),* [ASET]; *(with reflex.)* transport oneself 892[3]

āsittan, *v.(5),* [ASIT]; run aground

āþ, *m.a-stem,* OATH

āþīestrian, *w.v.(2),* [ATHESTER]; darken, be eclipsed 879

āweg, *adv.* AWAY

āweorpan, *v.(3),* [AWARP]; cast out, overthrow, 867

āwerian, *w.v.(1a),* protect 885[4]

Æ

æfter, *prep.w.dat.,* AFTER 855 &c; along, through 878[6], 893[11]

æghwæþer (887), **ǣgþer** (893), *pron.* EITHER; each

ǣgþer, *conj.; ǣ. ge . . . ge,* both . . . and 893[69]

ǣlc, *pron.* EACH; *mǣstra daga ǣlce,* almost every day 893[13]

ǣlc, *adj.* EACH, any, every 891

ælmesse, *f.n-stem,* ALMS 887[20]n

ǣniᵹ, *adj.* ANY 893[10]

ǣr, *adv.* ERE, before, formerly 836, 876; previously 880; before this 885[17]; for the first time 851; first 896[45]; **ǣrest,** *superl.* first 890

ǣr, *conj.* ERE, before 877, &c; *(w.subj.)* 836

ǣr, *prep.w.dat.* before 885[15]

ærcebiscep (870), **erce-** (888), *m.a-stem,* ARCHBISHOP

æsc, *m.a-stem,* warship 896[19]

æt, *prep.w.dat.* AT 833; of 887[6]; on 896[24]

ætēowan, *w.v.(1b),* [ATEW]; appear, show, 891[16]

ætgædere, *adv.* together

B

bāt, *m.a-stem,* BOAT 891

be, bī (893[11]), *prep.w.dat.* BY 857; by, on 878[15], &c; on, to 871[38]; at 885[34]; along 893[25], 895[9]

bēag, *m.a-stem,* [BEE]; armring, armlet, 876n

bearn, *n.a-stem,* [BAIRN]; child

beebbian, *w.v.(2),* strand (by the ebb tide) 896[40]

befæstan, *w.v.(1b),* secure, make safe 893[90]; entrust 886

bēgen, *adj.* [BO]; both 867 &c; **būtū** (*n.acc.*) 871[26]

begeondan, *prep.w.dat.* BEYOND

begietan, *v.(5)* [BEGET]; get; **begeton** (*p.t.pl.*) 896[3]

behindan, *adv.* BEHIND

behinon (878[17]), **behienan** (885[26]), *prep.w.dat.* on this side of

behorsian, *w.v.(2),* deprive of horses 885[6]

bēn, *f.i-stem,* [BENE]; request 885[34]

beniman, *v.(4),* [BENIM]; *(w. gen.)* deprive of 894[3]

bēon, *anom.v.* BE 891; **is,** *3sg.* is 878[27]; **sie,** *3sg.subj.* may be 891

berǣdan, *w.v.(1b),* deprive of 887[6]*

berōwan, *v.(7),* row past 896[48]

besittan, *v.(5),* [BESIT]; surround, besiege; **beseten,** *p.pt.* 893[64], 894[10]

bestelan, *v.(4),* [BESTEAL];
(*w.reflex. and followed by gen.*) steal away from, 865, 876n, &c

betst, *adj.superl.* BEST 891

betweox (867), **betweoh** (890), **betwuh** (893[8]), *prep.w.dat.* between, amongst

bi, see **be**

biddan, *v.(5),* BID; beg, pray 853

binnan, *adv.* [BIN]; within 867

binnan, *prep.w.dat.* within 895[19]

biscep (845), **biscop,** (870), *m.a-stem,* BISHOP; **biscepas,** *nom.pl.* 833

biscepsunu, *m.u-stem,* godson at confirmation, spiritual son, 853

bisceprīce, *n.ja-stem,* BISHOP-RIC, see, 867

bōcian, *w.v.(2),* [BOOK]; grant by charter 855

bōclǣden, *n.a-stem,* [BOCLEDEN] (literary) Latin 891

geboren, *p.pt.* BORN 887[11]

brād, *adj.* BROAD 892[8]

brecan, *v.(4),* BREAK 885[37]; attack, storm 851, 867

(ge)brengan, *w.v.(1b),* BRING 893[50], 895[10]

gebrocian, *w.v.(2),* destroy, crush 896[4]; **gebrocede,** *p.pt.pl.* 896[5]

brōður, *m.r-stem,* BROTHER 860, &c; (*g.sg.*) 887[5]

brycg, *f.jō-stem,* BRIDGE 887[1]

būan, *w.v.(3),* dwell; **būgeað,** *3pl.pres.* 893[34]; **būde,** *3sg.p.t.* 890

bufan, *prep.w.dat.* [BOVE]; above

burg, *f.monos-stem,* BOROUGH; city, fortified town; strong-hold, fort 893[15], (*g.sg.*) 895[7]

burgware, *f.ō-stem* (*pl.*), townsmen, citizens 893[42]

būtan, -on *prep.w.dat.* BUT; without 891, 893[25]; except (for), apart from, 878, 886[4]n; outside 893[97]

būtan, -on, *adv.* without, outside 867, 893[96]

būte, *conj.* BUT 896[23]

būton, *conj.* except that 889

būtū, see **bēgen**

C

cēap, *m.a-stem,* [CHEAP]; property, possessions, (*g.sg.*) 893[96]

ceaster, *f.ō-stem,* fort, city, 867 &c.

cēosan, *v.(2),* CHOOSE 890*, elect 870.

cirice, *f.n-stem,* CHURCH 874

cirlisc, *adj.* CHURLISH; common, rustic, 892[12]

cirr, *m.i-stem,* time, occasion 896[24]

gecirran, *w.v.(1b),* [I-CHERRE]; submit 878, 886; *to þam gecirdon,* resolved this 867; *to anum gecierdon,* united 835

cniht, *m.a-stem,* KNIGHT; boy 893[58]

corn, *n.a-stem,* CORN 893[98]

crismlīsing, *f.ō-stem,* baptism 878[29]n

Cristna, *m.n-stem,* CHRISTIAN; Englishman 893[85]

cuēn, *f.i-stem,* QUEEN 888; *hæfde to cuene,* had married 836, &c

cuman, *v.(4),* COME; *c. ute,* were outside 893[18]; *c. onweg,* escape 896[34]; **cuōm,** *p.t.sg.* 835 &c; **cōm** 855, 878[25]; **cuōmon,** *p.t.pl.* 891, **cōmon** 885[9]; **cōme,** *p.t.subj.* 893[56]

cumpæder, *m.a-stem,* fellow godfather, gossip, 893[60] (Lat. *compater*)

GLOSSARY

cweþan, *v.(5),* [QUETHE] ; say

cwild, *m. or f.i-stem,* death, mortality ; *ceapes* c.7 *monna,* murrain and plague, 896⁶

cynerīce, *n.ja-stem,* [KINNRICK] ; kingdom, realm 871³⁸

cyning, *m.a-stem,* KING 833 ; **kyning** 878²⁴ ; **cyng** 860, 893³⁸ ; **cinges** *(g.sg.)* 893⁷³

cynn, *n.ja-stem,* KIN ; race 893⁷⁶

D

dæg, *m.a-stem,* DAY, time, 851, 871²⁶

dæges, *adv.* by day 893⁹²

dǣl, *m.i-stem,* DEAL ; share, part,

gedǣlan, *w.v.(1b),* DEAL, share out, 876

Denisc, *adj.* DANISH ; the Danish pattern 896²³ ; *ða Deniscan,* the Danes 896³⁶

dēop, *n.a-stem,* the DEEP, channel, 896³⁶

dohtor, *f.r-stem,* DAUGHTER

dōn, *anom.v.* DO 853, 895¹¹

gedōn, *anom.v.* [I-DO] ; do 896²⁵ ; arrive 893⁷¹

drǣfan, *w.v.(1b),* [DREFE] ; drive 887¹⁸

dreccan, *w.v.(1b),* [DRETCH] ; oppress, harass 896¹⁵

drȳge, *adj.* DRY ; *on drygum,* on dry land 896³⁰

E

ēa, *f.ō-stem,* [EA] ; river, *(acc.)* 895¹⁰ ; **ēas,** *g.sg.* 895¹², **ē,** *g.sg.* 893⁸⁰* ; **ēi,** *d.sg.* 875 ; **ēæ** 895⁹

ēac, *prep.w.dat.* also, in addition to, 878²³, &c

ēaca, *m.n-stem,* [EKE] ; increase, reinforcement 893⁶⁹

ealdormon (893⁵⁵), **-man** (893⁷²), **aldormon** (837), **-man** (845), *m.monos-stem,* ALDERMAN, chief officer of a *scir,* 837n

eal(l), *n.a-stem,* ALL, everything, 893⁴⁹, *(w.gen.)* 893⁹⁶ ; *mid ealle,* and everything 892⁴, &c

eall, *adj., pron.* ALL, 890, 893⁵ ; **al,** *acc.n.sg.* 855 ; **all** 870 ; **alle,** *acc.f.sg.* 865 ; **alne,** *acc.m.sg.* 853 ; **alle,** *acc.pl.* 853 ; **allum,** *d.sg.* 860 ; *d.pl.* in *on allum þam,* with all those 874¹⁰

eall, *adv.* altogether 893⁹⁸ ; in its (their) entirety 893¹⁸

ealles, *adv.* altogether 896⁴

earc, *f.ō-stem,* ARK 855²⁷

ēas, see **ēa**

ēast, *adv.* in the EAST 886 ; eastward 891

ēastan, *adv.* from the east ; *be eastan,* on the east of 893⁷⁵

ēast-ende, *m.ja-stem,* EAST-END 892⁶

ēasteweard, *adj.* eastern 865

ēasteweardes, *adv.* to the east 893⁴⁰

ēastlang, *adv.* eastwards, extending east, 892⁷

ēast-rīce, *n.ja-stem,* the eastern kingdom, Austrasia, 892², 893²

ēastron, *f.n-stem (pl.),* EASTER

ēce, *adj.,* ECHE ; eternal 855

efenēhð(o), *f.ō-stem,* neighbourhood 893⁸⁹n

efes, *f.ō-stem,* EAVES ; edge, side, 893¹²

efor, *m.a-stem,* [EVER] ; wild boar 885¹⁶

eft, *adv.* [EFT.] ; again

ēi, see **ēa**

ende, *m.ja-stem,* END 893⁶⁰n

elþīodignes, *f.jō-stem,* pilgrimage 891

Englisc, *adj.* ENGLISH 896 ; the English language 891

eorl, *m.a-stem,* jarl 871²n

ercebiscop, see **ærcebiscep**

ergan, *w.v.(1a),* [EAR] ; plough 876

F

faran, *v.(6),* FARE, go 851 ; *(p.t.subj.pl.)* would go 876 ; *(reflex.)* went 855 ; *of f.* abandon 893²⁰

gefaran, *v.(6),* [IFARE] ; go, depart, 877 ; die 855, 867, &c

fæder, *m.r-stem,* FATHER

fædren-healf, *f.ō-stem),* paternal side 887¹⁰

gefægen, *adj.* FAIN ; glad *(w.gen.)* 855, 878¹⁸

fær, *n.a-stem,* FARE ; journey ; *on fære* on his way 893²⁹

færeld, *n.a-stem,* journey, pilgrimage 889

fæsten, *n.ja-stem,* stronghold, fortification 877, 885³

fēa, *adj.* FEW ; a few 892¹¹

feaxed, *ppt.,* [FAXED] ; longhaired, 891¹⁷

fela, *n.indecl. (orig.u-stem) w.gen.* [FELE] ; many 871¹⁹, &c

feld, *m.u-stem,* FIELD ; open country 893¹⁰n

fenn, *m.* or *n.ja-stem,* FEN 892¹²n.

feoh, *n.a-stem (orig.u-stem),* FEE ; goods, property, 865, 878³¹, &c

feoh-gehāt, *n.a-stem,* promise of money 865

feohlēas, *adj.* moneyless 896²

gefeoht, *n.a-stem,* FIGHT, battle, fighting, 868, &c

(ge)feohtan, *v.(3),* FIGHT 833, &c

feor, *adv.* FAR 882

feorh, *m.u-stem,* life 855¹⁵

fēorða, *adj.* FOURTH 851

fēower, *adj.* FOUR 882

fēowertig, *num.(w.gen.),* FORTY 893³⁶

gefēra, *m.n-stem,* [YFERE] ; companion, servant 878³⁰

fēran, *w.v.(1b),* [FERE] ; go, proceed, 835, &c

ferian, *w.v.(1a),* FERRY ; carry, transport 893²¹, 893³³

gefetian, *w.v.(2),* [YFET] ; fetch, take away ; **gefetedon** 895¹⁷

fierd (867), **fird** (894⁷), *f.i-stem,* [FERD] ; levy, army, esp. West Saxon army, 835, &c ; *d.sg.* from the army 876

fierdian, *w.v.(2),* serve, be on military service, 893³⁰

fierdlēas, *adj.* without army, unguarded, 893¹²

fīf, *num.* FIVE 896³³

flēam, *m.a-stem,* [FLEME] ; flight 893⁸⁷

flēon, *v.(2),* FLEE 893²⁵

geflīeman, *w.v.(1b),* [FLEME] ; put to flight, drive away, 835, &c ; *(p.pt.pl.)* 871¹⁹

flocc, *m.a-stem,* FLOCK ; troop 893¹³

flocrād, *f.ō-stem,* gang, troop 893¹²

flōd, *f. ō-stem,* FLOOD ; tide 896⁴⁵

folc, *n.a-stem,* FOLK 878 ; body of men 893⁴⁰

folc-gefeoht, *n.a-stem,* battle 871³⁷, 887¹⁶

fōn, *v.(7),* [FANG] ; seize, receive, get ; *feng to rice,* succeeded to (took) the throne 836, &c

gefōn, *v.(7),* [IFANG] ; take, seize 851, 893²¹

for, *prep.* FOR, through, 891 ; 893⁹n

foran, *adv.* [FORNE] ; from in front 893²³

forbærnan, *w.v.(1b),* [FORBURN] ; burn up 893⁵¹

foregīsl, *m.a-stem,* (preliminary) hostage 877, &c

foresprecen, *p.pt.* [FORESPOK-EN] ; 885¹, 895¹

forfaran, *v.(6),* obstruct 896²⁷

forhergian, *w.v.(2),* ravage 887¹⁷

forlǣtan, *v.(7),* [FORLET] ; leave, abandon, 885⁶, 895¹⁴

forrīdan, *v.(1),* ride before ; intercept, cut off, 893²³, 893⁹⁷

forslægen, *p.pt.* slain 882

forswīðe, *adv.* utterly 896⁴

forþ, *adv.* FORTH, forward, on, 887¹⁸, 893⁴¹

forþǣm, *conj.* because 887¹⁰, &c

forþfēran, *w.v.(1b),* depart, die

forþon þe, *conj.* because 891

forðȳ ðe, *conj.* [FORTHY] ; be-cause 894³, 896³⁴

forweorþan, *v.(3),* [FORWORTH] ; perish, be lost, 877, &c

forwiernan, *w.v.(1b),* FORWARN ; withhold, deny, 895⁸

forwundian, *w.v.(2),* [FOR-WOUND] ; wound 882, 896⁵¹

forwyrcan, *w.v.(1b),* [FOR-WORK] ; obstruct, barricade, 895¹⁰

fram (892¹¹), **from** (872), *prep. w.dat.* FROM ; by 838

gefrēogan, *w.v.(2),* *orig.(3),* [YFREE] ; befriend, honour 885³³

Frēsisc, *adj.* Frisian 896⁴³ ; the Frisian pattern 896²²

fretan, *v.(5),* [FRET] ; eat, eat to the bone 893⁸²

frettan, *w.v.(1b),* eat, eat bare 893⁹⁸

friþ, *m.a-stem* *(orig.u-stem),* [FRITH] ; peace, *friþ nam* made peace 876, &c

from, see **fram**

fulluht-nama, *m.n-stem,* bap-tismal name 890

fulnēah, *adv.* FULL NIGH, almost 896¹⁹

fultum, *m.a-stem,* [FULTUM] ; help 893⁴²

(ge)fultumian, *w.v.(2),* help, support, 836, &c ; *(p.t.subj.)* 853

fulwiht, *n.a-stem* *(orig.f.i-stem),* [FULLOUGHT] ; baptism 878²⁴

furlang, *n.a-stem,* FURLONG 896³⁸

furþum, *adv.* [FORTHEN] ; al-ready, just, 895¹²

gefylce, *n.ja-stem,* troop, divi-sion, 871¹² ; *d.pl.* 871²⁵

gefyrn, *adv.* [FERN] ; before, formerly, 892²

G

gegadrian, *w.v.(2),* GATHER 867

gān, *anom.v.* GO 885⁵, &c. See **hond**

gegān, *anom.v.* [IGO] ; subdue, overrun, 870, 874

gangdagas, *m.a-stem* *(pl.)* [GANGDAYS] ; Rogation Days 891

ge, *conj.* [YE] ; *ge . . . ge . . .* both . . . and . . . 835, &c

gēar, *n.a-stem,* YEAR 836, &c ; *gere (d.sg.)* 894¹ ; *ger (acc. pl.)* 894¹⁶

gearo, *adj.* [YARE] ; ready for, prepared for, 874

giefan, *v.(5),* GIVE ; give in marriage 853, 855

gif, *conj.* IF 893¹⁰

gifu, *f.ō-stem,* [GIVE] ; gift 885³⁵

gioncg, *adj.* YOUNG, *(as byname)* 871¹⁸

gīsl, *m.a-stem,* [YISEL] ; hostage 874

God, *m.a-stem,* GOD 855

gōd, *adj.* GOOD 860 ; considerable 837

godsunu, *m.u-stem,* GODSON 890

H

habban, *w.v.(3),* HAVE *(auxil.)* 836, &c ; possess, hold 867 ; marry 885[30]

haldan, see **healdan**

hālga, *m.n-stem,* saint ; *ealra haligra mæssa,* All Hallows' Day 900 ; **halechen** *(d.pl.)* 890

(ge)hālgian, *w.v.(2),* HALLOW, consecrate 853, 887[8]

hālig, *adj.* HOLY 876

hām, *m.a-stem,* HOME 893[16]

hāmweard, *adv.* HOMEWARD, home, 855, &c.

hāmweardes, *adv.* HOMEWARDS ; on its way home 893[31]

(ge)hātan, *v.(7),* [*HIGHT*] ; name, call, 891, &c ; promise 865[2] ; bid, command, 896

gehāwian, *w.v.(2),* observe, notice, 895[9]

hæftnīede, *f.i-stem,* domination, custody, 886

hǣlo, *f.īn-stem,* [*HEAL*] ; salvation 855 *(d.sg.)*

hærfest, *m.a-stem,* HARVEST, autumn, 877, 895[6]

hǣt, from **hātan**

hǣþen, *adj.* HEATHEN ; *hæþne men,* the Scandinavians 832, &c

hē, *pron.m.* HE 835 ; **hine** (836), **hiene** (853), *acc.* him 853, it 878[20], 891 *(reflex.)* 865, &c ; **his,** *gen.* of him 878[17], his 836, &c ; **him,** *dat.* him 838, &c, it 878[20], to him, his 885[31], 893[54], *(reflex.)* 855,

&c ; **hire,** *f.gen.* her 888, **hiere,** of it 878[17]n ; **hit,** *n,* it 860, 877 (cf **sum**)

healdan (860), **haldan** (874, 886), *v.(7),* HOLD, keep, rule.

healf, *f.ō-stem,* HALF ; side 887[15]

healf, *adj.* HALF, *(n.pl.)* 893[16] ; *oþrum (þridde, feorðe) healfum* one (two, three) and a half 851, 900, &c

hefelīc, *adj.* [HEAVILY] ; heavy, serious, hard, 868

hēr, *adv.* HERE ; at this place in the annals 832, &c

here, *m.ja-stem,* [HERE] ; band of robbers ; the Danish army 837[5]n ; **herige** (838), **here** (875), *d.sg.* ; **heres** 878[10]n.

herehȳþ, *f.i-stem,* booty, plunder, 885, 893[21]

hergian, *w.v.(2),* HARROW ; plunder, seize, 875, &c

hergaþ, *m.a-stem (orig.u-stem,* harrying, plundering raid, 893[47]

hider, *adv.* HITHER 893[100]

hīe, *pron.pl.* they 835, 882 ; **hī** 887[9] ; **hīe,** *acc.* them 871[3], 896[29] ; **hī** 891 ; *(reflex.)* 876[5], 891 ; **hiora** 892[10], **heora** 893[6], **hiera** 867, **hira** 896[40], *gen.* of them 875, &c, their 867, theirs 896[46], *(obj.)* them 893[55] ; *(reflex.)* for themselves 876n ; **him,** *dat.* (for) them 835, 896[28] ; *(reflex.)* for themselves 896[3]

hīera, *adj.comp.* HIGHER 896[21]

hīeran, *w.v.(1b),* HEAR 851, &c

gehīersum, *adj.* [HEARSUM] ; submissive, obedient 853

hīersumian, *w.v.(2),* [HEARSUM] ; make obedient, subject, *(p.t.subj.)* 853

hindan, *adv.* in the rear, from behind, 877, 893[78]

hléapere, *m.ja-stem,* courier, messenger, 889

hlōþ, *f.ō-stem,* band (of robbers) 879, 893[11]n

hond, *f.u-stem,* HAND ; side 853, 871[8] ; *to his honda,* at his hand, of him 887[9] ; *on hond eodon* submitted, surrendered to 882

hors, *n.a-stem,* HORSE 892[4]

hors-þegn, *m.a-stem,* horse-thane, marshal 896[13], 896[53]

gehorsud, -od, *p.pt.* [YHORSED]; supplied with horses, mounted, 866, &c

hrǣdlíce, *adv.* [RADLY] ; quickly 876

hund, *num.* [HUND] ; hundred 851, (892[5])

hundtwelftig, *num.* (*n.a-stem*), hundred and twenty 892[7]

hungor, *m.a-stem* (*orig.u-stem*), HUNGER 893[83]

hwǣr, *conj.* WHERE 895[9]

hwǣr, *adv.* WHERE 891

gehwæþer, hwaþer, *adj.* WHETHER ; which 893[12] ; either, each, 853, 871[7]

hwelc, *adj.* WHICH ; *swa hwelc* whatsoever 874

hwíl, *f.ō-stem,* WHILE, time, 837 ; *þa hwile þe . . . lengest* as long as 893[27]

hwílum, *adv.* WHILOM, at times, sometimes, 891

hȳd, *f.i-stem,* HIDE, skin, 891

I

ic, *pron.* I 893[64]

íggað, *m.a-stem,* [AIT] ; island 893[26]

ígland, *n.a-stem,* ISLAND 894[9]

ilca, *adj.* [ILK] ; same

in, *adv.* IN 893[22]

in, *prep.w.dat.* IN, amongst, 878[26], 893[34]

innan, *prep.w.acc.* [INNE] ; **in,** into, 868, &c

inne, *adv.* [INNE] ; within, inside, 867, &c.

intō, *prep.w.dat.* INTO 876, &c

L

lāf, *f.ō-stem,* [LAVE] ; remainder 867, &c

lang, *adj.* LONG 891 ; **lengra,** *comp.* 892[8] ; **lengest,** *superl. adv.* 893[27] (see **hwíl**)

langscip, *n.a-stem,* warship 896[19]

lārēow, *m.wa-stem,* [LAREW] ; teacher 891

late, *adv.* LATE 867

(ge)lǣdan, *w.v.(1b),* LEAD, take, convey, 871[6], &c

lǣs, *adv.* LESS 900

lǣstan, *w.v.(1b),* [LAST] ; follow, serve, 874

gelǣstan, *w.v.(1b),* [YLAST]; do, perform, 878[24]

gelend, *p.pt.* landed, arrived 886 ; gone 893[61]

lengra, lengest, see **lang**

lēod, *f.ō-stem,* [LEDE] ; (*in pl.*) people 855

lēoma, *m.n-stem,* [LEAM] ; beam of light 891

líc, *n.a-stem,* [LICH] ; body, corpse, 855, 860, &c

licgan, *v.(5),* LIE, rest ; **líþ,** *3sg.pres.* 855, &c ; *lið ut,* flows out 892[9]

lof, *n.a-stem,* [LOF] ; praise, glory, 855

gelōme, *adv.* [YLOME] ; frequently 887[16]

lond, *n.a-stem,* LAND 855, &c ; district 870

longe, *adv.* LONG, for a long time 871[26]

lufu, *f.ō-stem,* LOVE 891[7]n

lȳtel, *adj.* LITTLE, small, (*instr. sg.*) 871³⁵, 878⁶n

M

mā, *sb.indecl.* more 896²⁰

manig, see monig

mæsse, *f.n-stem*, MASS, feast, 900

mǣst, *adj.superl.* MOST 893¹³ ; greatest 851 ; greater 878

meahte (877), mehte, *pret.- pres.*(5), could 893¹⁰ ; (*subj.*) MIGHT 896⁴⁵ ; *mehte to, to mehte*, could get to, could reach, 877, 896³⁷

mētan, *w.v.*(1b), MEET, come up, 868, 877, &c

gemētan, *w.v.*(1b), meet, oppose, 871³

mete, *m.i-stem*, MEAT ; food, provisions, 891, 893²⁷

metelīest, *f.i-stem*, lack of food, famine, 893⁸²

micel, *sb.w.gen.* much, a great part, 878

micel, *adj.* [MICKLE] ; big, great

micle, *adv.* much 896⁵

miclum, *adv.* greatly 878³⁰, 882

mid, *prep.w.dat.* [MID] ; with, along with 851, &c ; accompanied by 835, &c. See sē

mid, *adv.* with them, present, 885²⁵, 893⁶

mid(d), *adj.* MID 878, &c

middelrīce, *n.ja-stem*, middle kingdom 887¹³

mīl, *f.jō-stem*, MILE 892⁸

mon, *m.monos-stem*, MAN 832, 878¹⁰n

mon, *indef.pron.* ONE 871⁴¹, &c

mōnaþ, *m.þ-stem*, MONTH, 836, &c

monig (838), manig (896¹⁴), *pron.* MANY

monig, *adj.* MANY, many a, 853, &c

mōrfæsten, *n.ja-stem*, moor-stronghold 878

munt, *m.a-stem*, mountain, (*pl.*) Alps 887¹⁵

mūþa, *m.n-stem*, mouth (of a river), estuary, 845, &c

N

nā, *adv.* NO ; not, never, 893⁹⁴ ; *na ne*, not at all, never 871⁴¹

nān, *pron.* NONE 887¹⁰, 896³⁷

nān, *adj.* NO 868, &c

nāwðer, *conj.* [NAUTHER] ; *nawðer ne . . . ne*, neither . . . nor 896²²

næfde, *3sg.p.t.* had not 896³

næs, *3sg.p.t.* was not 887¹⁰, &c ; nǣron, *pl.* were not 896²²

ne, *adv.* not 871⁴¹, &c

nēah, *adv.* NIGH, near 894¹¹ ; nīehst, *superl.* nearest 878¹³, 893⁸n

genēat, *m.a-stem*, [GENEAT] ; follower, dependant, 896⁴³n

nēawest, *f.i-stem*, neighbourhood 895⁶

nemnan, *w.v.*(1b), [NEMN] ; call, name, mention, 891, &c

nerian, *w.v.*[1a], save, rescue 893⁸⁸

nīehst, see nēah

nigon, *num.* NINE 896²⁷

nigontēoþa, *adj.* NINETEENTH 855 (cf healf)

niht, *f.monos-stem*, NIGHT, night-time, 865, &c

nihtes, *adv.* by night 876, &c

niman, *v.*(4), [NIM] ; take 876, &c ; adopt 853 ; *sige nom*, won the victory 837, &c

geniman, *v.*(4), take, seize, capture, 882

nīwe, *adj.* NEW 896²⁷

nōlǣs, adv.(as sb.), no less 896[51]

noldon, 3pl. would not do 876

nōm, see **niman**

norþ, adv. NORTH 893[36]

norþan, adv. from the North ; be *norþan* on the north of 893[75]

norþerne, adj. NORTHERN 890

norþsǣ, f.i-stem, the Bristol Channel 893[37]n

norþweardes, adv. NORTHWARDS 893[21]

genotud, p.pt. used up 893[29]n

nytwyrðe, adj. useful 896[23]

O

of, prep.w.dat. OF, by 890 ; out of, from 836, &c ; *þær . . . of* therefrom 891

of, adv. OFF, away, 896[30]

ofer, prep.w.acc. OVER, through, 851, &c ; throughout 855 ; across 867, &c ; beyond, after, 853, 878 ; contrary to 893[4] ; after 871[30]

ofer, adv. across 892[4]

oferhergan, w.v.(2), overrun 865 ; oferhergeadon 832

offaran, v.(6), pursue, overtake. 893[77], 893[94]

ofrīdan, v.(1), overtake 877

ofslēan, v.(6), [OFSLAY] ; slay 837, 871[20]

oft, adv. OFT, often, 875* ; oftor, comp. more often 893[18]

on, adv. ON ; therein 892[12]

on, prep.w.acc. ON 871[41], &c ; into 836, &c ; against 835 ; in accordance with 896[22] ; w.dat. on 887[10] ; in, amongst, 838, &c ; inside 868 ; in, during 860[4], 865, &c

ond (894[1]), conj. AND 853, &c ; but 837, 871[36], &c ; usually by the ampersand 7

onlong (882), **andlang** (887[2]) prep.w.gen. ALONG

ondweard, adj. present 851*

onforan, prep.w.acc. [AFORE] ; before, at the beginning, 893[90]

onfōn, v.(7), [ONFANG] ; receive 878[28], 893[55] (w.gen.)

ongēan, prep.w.acc. against, to, to meet, 893[22] ; **ongēn** 878[16], 896[19]

ongietan, v.(5), [ANGET] ; perceive ; onget 895[13]

onginnan, v.(3), [ONGIN] ; begin 895[12]

onwald, m.a-stem, [ONWALD] ; rule, dominion, 900

onweg, adv. AWAY 896[34]*

oþ, prep.w.acc. until, up to, 851 ; to, as far as, up to, 868, &c

ōþer, pron. OTHER ; the other(s) 875, &c ; the rest 851, 893[83] ; oþer . . . oþer, (the) one . . . the other 871[12], 893[54]

ōþer, adj. OTHER 892[15] ; another, second, 885[3], 893[61] ; oþer . . . oþer, one . . . the other 885[2], 893[19]

oðrōwan, v.(7), row away 896[46]

oþþæt, conj. until 885[4], &c

oþþe, conj. until 893[41] ; or 891 ; oþþe . . . oþþe, either . . . or 893[51]

oðwindan, v.(3), escape 896[32]

P

pāpa, m.n-stem, POPE 885[33]

R

rād, f.ō-stem, [ROAD] ; raid 871[41]

gerǣcan, w.v.(1b), REACH, deal with, 893[10] ; overtake 894[7] ; capture 885[11]

ræde, *adj.* mounted 891

rædlíce, *adv.* [REDLY] ; skilfully 887[17]

reccan, *w.v.(1b),* RECK, care, *(p.t.pl.)* 891

geréfa, *m.n-stem,* REEVE 896[42]*n

geréþru, *n.(pl.)* steering gear 891

ríce, *n.ja-stem,* [RICHE] ; kingdom, dominion, authority, throne, 836, &c

rícsian, *w.v.(2),* rule 836, &c

rídan, *v.(1),* RIDE 870, &c

gerídan, *v.(1),* *tr.* override, occupy, 878[2], 878[4] ; *intr.* ride 878[14]

ríman, *w.v.(1b),* [RIME] ; count 871

ríp, *n.(a-stem),* [RIPE] ; crop, harvest, 895[8]

ród, *f.ó-stem,* ROOD, cross, 885[36]

róhton, see **reccan**

rýmet, *n.ja-stem,* room, space, 893[8]

gerýpan, *v.(1),* [RIPE] ; reap 895[7]

S

salde, see **sellan**

same, *adv.* likewise 891[17]n

samnian, *w.v.(2),* [SAM] ; gather, muster, 893[19]

samworht, *p.pt.* half-constructed 892[13]

sárgian, *w.v.(2),* WOUND 896[47]

sǽ, *f.i-stem,* SEA 874, &c

sǽ-rima, *m.n-stem,* [SEARIM] ; sea-shore 896[26]

gescæpen, *p.pt.* shaped, built, 896[22]

sceoldon, *3pl.p.t.* SHOULD 887[10] ; **scolden** *(subj.)* were to 893[17]

scip, *n.a-stem,* SHIP 851 ; **scipo,** *acc.pl.* 885[11]

sciphere, *m.ja-stem,* fleet, esp. the Danish fleet 835, &c ; the English fleet 875

sciphlæst, *m.a-stem,* ship-load, crew, 833, &c

scipian, *w.v.(2),* SHIP, embark 892[3]

scír, *f.ó-stem,* SHIRE ; division (of the army) 893[30]

scól, *f.ó-stem,* SCHOOL, hostel, 874n, 885[34]

scolden, see **sceoldon**

sé, *dem.pron.* that, it ; **þá,** *acc. f.sg.* it 893[21] ; **þæt,** *n.nom.* that, it 887[8], &c, *acc.* 835 ; 7 **þæt,** which 878[27] ; **þæs,** *g.sg.* of it, of him, 855 ; **þǽm,** *n.dat.sg.* that, it, 894[1], 896[33], **þám** 855 ; *tó þǽm,* to such an extent 896[47] ; *mid þǽm þæt,* in that *(conj.)* 896[6] ; **þá,** *n.pl.* these 896[33], those, the latter 882, 893[37], 893[40] ; *acc.pl.* them 885[10] ; **þám,** *d.pl.* 871[39], 874. Often indistinguishable (as 885[17], &c) from

sé, *rel.pron.m.* who 885[29], which 878[13] ; **þæs,** *g.sg.* whose 890 ; **sío,** *f.n.sg.* who 888, **séo** which 893[93] ; **þæt,** *neut.n.sg.* which 886, 890, &c

sé, *dem.adj.m.* this, that, 836, &c ; **þæs,** *neut.g.sg.* þæs geares that year 871[37], þæs ilcan wintra, in that same winter 878[7] ; **þá,** *f.acc.sg.* 887[14] ; **þá,** *n.pl.* those 882, often indistinguishable from

sé, *def.art.m.* the 833, &c ; **þone,** *acc.sg.* 837 ; **þæs,** *g.sg.* 871[39] ; **þám,** *d.sg.* 838, **þǽm** 892[9] ; **séo,** *f.nom.sg.* 892[9], **sío** 879 ; **ðá,** *f.acc.sg.* 885[3] ; **þǽre,** *f.g.sg.* 885[36] ; **þǽre,** *f.d.sg.* 867, 885[12] ; **þæt,** *neut. sg.* 896[32] ; *acc.* 851, &c ; **þæs,** *neut.g.sg.* 894[3] ; **þám,** *neut.d.sg.* 868 ; **þý,** *neut.instr.*

sg. 871[38] ; **þā,** *n.pl.* 881 ;
þāra, *g.pl.* 893[82] ; **þǣm,**
d.pl. 893[41]

sēcan, *w.v.(1b),* SEEK, make for,
867, 893[10]

secgan, *w.v.(3),* SAY, tell, 851 ;
sǣde *1sg.pret.* 893[64]

self, *adj.* SELF 855, &c

sellan, *w.v.(1b),* SELL ; give,
grant, 893[56] ; **salde** 836, 874 ;
saldon 877, **sealdon** 874

sendan, *w.v.(1b),* SEND 853

seofon, *num.adj.* SEVEN 891

seofoða, *adj.* SEVENTH 878[14]

set, *n.a-stem,* habitation, camp,
893[18]

gesettan, *w.v.(1a),* SET ; build,
restore, 886

sex (896[25]), **syx** (900) *num.adj.*
SIX

sibsumnes, *f.jō-stem,* [SIB-
SOMENESS] ; peace 860

simle, *adv.* always, constantly,
893[16]

sīo, see **sē**

sige, *m.i-stem,* [SIƷE] ; victory

sigelan, *w.v.(1b),* SAIL 877

sittan, *v.(5),* SIT, remain, stay,
851, &c

gesittan, *v.(5),* settle, remain,
874, 879 ; *(p.pt.)* stayed,
finished, 893[28]n

sīþ, *m.a-stem,* [SITHE] ; journey
892[4] ; time, occasion, 893[19]

siþþan, *adv.* [SITHEN] ; after-
wards 893[11]

slēan, *v.(6),* SLAY ; *micel wæl
geslog,* &c, made great slaughter 837, &c

sōna, *adv.* SOON 885[7]

standan, *v.(6),* STAND, be, 891,
896[29]

stælhere, *m.ja-stem,* predatory
band 896[17]

stælwyrð, *adj.* [STALWORTH] ;
serviceable 895[18]

stæþ, *n.a-stem,* STAITH ; (river-)
bank 893[78] ; shore, sea-shore,
896[16]

stede, *m.i-stem,* STEAD, place 887

stemn, *m.(a-stem),* period of service 893[28]

steorra, *m.n-stem,* STAR 891

sum, *adj.* SOME, a, 893[35], &c ;
one 895[8] ; *hie sume,* some of
them 867, *hit sum,* some of it
877, *sumum þam here,* part of
the army 875

sum, *pron.* one 878[26]n ; some
877

sumor, *m.u-stem,* SUMMER 875

sumorlida, *m.n-stem,* summer
army 871[30]n

sunne, *f.n-stem,* SUN 879

sunu, *m.u-stem,* SON 851

sūþ, *adv.* SOUTH 851

sūþan, *adv.* from the south ; *be
suþan* to the south of 871[38]

sūð-rima, *m.n-stem,* south
coast 896[52]

sūð-stæð, *n.a-stem,* south coast
896[16]

swā, *adv.* SO, in such a way,
853, 878[25], &c ; *swa hwaþerre
swa,* whichever 893[12] ; *eac
swa,* likewise, moreover, 895[3] ;
7 eac swa, and so he did also
893[57]

swā, *conj.* as, even as, 885[27] ;
swa . . . swa, so (as) . . .
as 874, &c ; *swa swa,* so that
894[7] ; *sona swa,* as soon as
885[9]

sweostor, *f.r-stem,* sister 888

swerian, *v.(6),* SWEAR 874

swift, *adj.* SWIFT 896[21]

swīðe, *adv.* [SWITH] ; greatly
896[16] ; very 893[40] ; **swīþor,**
comp. more, more severely,
896[5] ; *superl.* in *ealles swiþost,
ealra swiþust,* most of all
896[6], 896[17]

T

tēon, *v.(2)*, [TEE] ; draw, tow, 892[10], 894[15]

tēoþa, *adj.* TENTH 855

tīd, *f.i-stem*, TIDE ; hour 879

tilian, *w.v.(2)*, TILL ; gain a livelihood 876n

timbran, *w.v.(1b)*, build 898[18]

tō, *prep.w.acc.* TO 836 ; *w.gerund* 886 ; *w.dat.* to 885 ; to, for, 855, 874 ; as 836, 885[21] ; see **hond**

tō, *adv.* TO ; thereto 887[8] ; up 893[48] ; forth 896[27]

tōbrecan, *v.(5)*, [TOBREAK] ; break up, break in pieces, 893[51], &c

tōcuman, *v.(4)*, come, arrive, 893[45]

tōdǣlan, *w.v.(1b)*, separate, divide, 885[1], 887[7]

tōfaran, *v.(6)*, disperse, scatter, 896[1]

tōniman, *v.(4)*, divide, split, 893[16]

trēow, *f.wō-stem*, pledge, treaty, 893[5]

getruma, *m.n-stem*, troop 871[15]

tū, *adv.* twice 896[19]

tū, see **twēgen**

tugon, see **tēon**

tūn, *m.a-stem*, TOWN ; enclosure 867n

tuwwa, *adv.* twice 893[18]

twēgen, **tuēgen**, *num.(adj.)m.* TWAIN, two, 833, &c ; **twā**, *neut.* 885[23], **tū** 882, 887[3] ; **twǣm**, *dat.* 871[12], **twām** 887[4]

twelf, *num.adj.* TWELVE 893[1]

tuelfta, *adj.* TWELFTH 878

þ

þā, *adv.* [THO] ; then 835[3], 851[10]

þā, *conj. þa . . .þa* when 885[11], 893[30]

þā, see **sē**

geþafung, *f.ō-stem*, consent, acquiescence 887[8]

þāra, *adv.* there 887[3]

þara, see **sē**

þǣr, *adv.* THERE 833, &c

þǣr, *conj.* where, 877, 893[8]

þǣron, *adv.* THEREON 882

þǣrtō, *adv.* thereby 895[13]

þæs, *adv.* after 871[30], *þæs on Eastron* the Easter after 878[10], *þæs ymb iii niht* three nights after 871[2]

þæs þe, *conj.* from the time when, after 855[9], 874

þæs, see **sē**

þæt, *conj.* THAT, so that 853

þæt, see **sē**

þe, *rel.pron.* who, that, which, 851, 871[39] ; whom 885[30] ; that, in which, when, 885[19], &c ; where 896[36] ; *þe . . . his*, whose 885[20]

þe, *conj.* than 900

þe, *part.* see **forþon**, **þæs**, &c

þēah, *adv.* however, nevertheless 867, &c ; **þēh** 896[45]

þearf, *f.ō-stem*, [THARF] ; profit, advantage, 874

þegn, *m.a-stem*, THANE 871[40]n ; **þēna** (*g.pl.*) 896[7]

þēh, *conj.* though 896[14]. See **þēah**

þēod, *f.ō-stem*, [THEDE] ; people, 867

þes, *dem.adj.* THIS ; **þisne**, *m.acc.sg.* 851 ; **þissum**, *d.sg.* 871[29], 889 ; **þysum** 892[1], 896[1] ; **þȳs**, *instr.sg.* 893[1], 894[1] ; **þisse**, *f.d.sg.* 885[27]

þiderweardes, *adv.* THITHERWARDS, thither ; on his way there 893[29]

þisse, see **þes**

þonces, adv. THANKS ; by the mercy 896[4]

þonne, adv. THEN 893[6] ; conj. than 893[18]

þonon, conj. [THENNE] ; whence 891

þrēo, see þrīe

þridda, adj. THIRD ; þ. fæder great-grandfather 885[27] ; see healf

þrīe, num.adj. THREE 891 ; þrēo, neut. 895[22] ; þrīm, dat. 896[5]

þrītig, adj. THIRTY 878[26]

þrōwian, w.v.(2), [THROW] ; suffer 885[36]

geþungen, p.pt.(as sb.) distinguished ; superl. 896[14]

þurh, prep.w.acc. THROUGH 887[1]

þus, adv. THUS 891

þūsend, num. THOUSAND 871[20]

geþuærness, f.jō-stem, concord, peace, 860

þȳ, conj. because ; þy . . . þy therefore . . . because 836

þȳ, see sē

þyncan, w.v.(1b), impers.w.dat. [THINK] ; seem 896[23]

þys(um), see þes

U

ufeweard, adj. higher, inner, 896[29]

ufor, adv.comp. further up 881

under, prep. UNDER, under cover of, 865, 876

underfōn, v.(7), [UNDERFO] ; take, accept, 867

uneðelīce, see unīeþelīce

ungecynd, adj. not of royal birth, low-born 867

ungemetlic, adj. immense 867

ungeþuærnes, f.jō-stem, discord, dissension, 867

unīeþelīce, adv. with difficulty 878 ; uneðelīce, awkwardly 896[35]

unsibb, f.jō-stem, enmity, hostility, 887[15]

unwealt, adj. steady 896[21]

unwīs, adj. UNWISE, foolish 874

up, adv. UP 860

uppe, adv. up 896[30]

ūt, adv. OUT 875

ūtan, adv. from without, outside, 893[27], &c ; without, to (on) the outside 885[5], 896[47]

ūte, adv. out 894[9] ; outside 893[18] ; out (on service) 893[17]

ūtermere, m.i-stem, outer waters, open sea, 896[28]

ūteweard, adj. OUTWARD ; outer 892[11], 896[32]

W

gewald, m.a-stem, [WIELD] ; power, control, command, 833 &c

gewalden, adj. small, inconsiderable 893[40]n

gewǣgd, p.pt. distressed, troubled, 893[82]

wæl, n.a-stem, [WAL] ; slaughter

wælsliht, m.i-stem, slaughter 839

wælstōw, f. wō-stem, place of slaughter, battlefield ; ahton wælstowe gewald, gained possession of the battlefield, won the battle, 833, &c

wæs, p.t.sg. WAS 838 ; was 853, &c ; remained 878[17] ; wǣron, pl. 835n, wǣrun 855 ; wǣre, subj.sg. was, might be 893[20], should be 874

wæter, n.a-stem, WATER 896[38]

wæter-fæsten, n.ja-stem, river-camp 893[9]

wē, pron. WE 851, 892[2]

weald, m.u-stem, WEALD, forest, 892[10]n

Wealhgerēfa, m.n-stem, the Welsh reeve 896[54]*n

wel, adv. WELL ; much 893[57]

welhwǣr, *adv.* almost everywhere 896²⁶

wendan, *w.v.(1b), often w.reflex.* WEND ; turn, go, return, 885¹²

geweorc, *n.a-stem,* (military) WORK, encampment, 868, &c ; gewerc 895¹⁶

weorpan, *v.(3),* [WARP] ; cast 896⁴⁸

weorþan, *v.(3),* [WORTH] ; be, become (*esp.w.p.pt.*) 833, &c

weorðian, *w.v.(2),* [WORTH] ; honour 878³¹

weorþness, *f.jō-stem,* honour, dignity, 855

weorþust, *adj.superl.* most honourable 878²⁷

wered, *n.a-stem,* [WERED] ; troop 871³⁵n

west, *adv.* WEST 876 ; wæst, in the west 893⁶⁶

westan, *adv.* from the west 893⁴²; *be westan,* on the west of, 893⁷⁴

west-dǣl, *m.i-stem,* western part 887¹³

wēste, *adj.* [WESTE] ; deserted, desolate, 893⁹²n

westlang, *adv.* westwards, extending west 892⁷

west-rīce, *n.ja-stem,* western kingdom 885¹⁹

westweard, *adv.* WESTWARD 892²

wīc, *f.* or *n.* (*in pl.*) camp 878¹⁹

wica, see wiece

wīceng, *m.a-stem,* viking, 879

wīc-gerēfa, *m.n-stem,* townreeve, bailiff, 896¹³*

(ge)wīcian, *w.v.(2),* [WICK] ; encamp, be encamped 893⁷

wiece, *f.n-stem,* WEEK 878²⁵; wiecan, *d.sg.* 878¹⁴; wucena, *g.pl.* 893⁸⁰; wicum, *d.pl.* 887⁶

wīf, *n.a-stem,* WIFE, woman, 893⁵³

winnan, *v.(3),* WIN ; fight, struggle, 835, 878¹²

winter, *m.u-stem,* WINTER, year 833, 836, &c

winter-setl, *n.a-stem,* winterquarters 866

wiota, *m.n-stem* [WITE] ; adviser, councillor 853

gewītan, *v.(1),* [WITE³] ; turn, go, 885⁷

wiþ, *prep.w.acc.* WITH ; against 837, 882, &c, (*after pron.*) 835, 851 ; *w.gen.* to, towards, 893³⁹; *w.dat.* with 865 ; against, in return for, 865 ; by, near 878²⁷

wolde, *p.t.* WOULD 877 ; *pl.* 874 ; wished, desired, 891, 893²⁰; (*subj.*) would wish to 874 ; would go 878²³

gewrit, *n.a-stem,* [IWRIT] ; letter 889

wucena, see wiece

wudu, *m.u-stem,* WOOD 892⁶

wudu-fæsten, *n.ja-stem,* the forest encampment 893⁹

gewundod, *p.pt.* wounded 893³²

wunian, *w.v.(2),* [WONE] ; dwell, remain, 855, 887¹¹

wyrcan, *w.v.(1b),* WORK ; make, build, construct, 878, &c ; geworct, *p.pt.* 893⁵⁹

Y

yfel, *n.a-stem,* EVIL, harm, 896²⁵

ymb, *prep.w.acc.* [UMBE] ; about 855, 874 ; after 891 ; around 885³

ymbe, *prep.w.acc.* about 891, 892²

ymbsittan, *v.(5),* besiege, surround, 885²

ymbūtan, *adv.* about ; *west y.* along the coast westward 877 ; 893³⁵

yst, *f.i-stem,* storm 877

INDEX OF PLACE-NAMES

71